REVIEWS FOR

Called to Truth

When asked to read this masterfully created piece, I didn't expect to finally discover a writing that completely exposes such a direct path to victory in Christ. This book caters to both the devoted life-long Christian and those who count today as the first day of their journey with Christ. Much of life is spent at war with the symptoms of a root cause. If you want to get to the bare root of what's been holding you back, this is the book for you. I would vehemently encourage Christian leaders to access the keys provided within these pages and not only experience personal growth, but watch the people you love finally blossom into who God intended them to be! — Pastor David Jordan, NOW Church, Plainfield, Illinois

First of all, let me start out by saying something about the Author. Denise White is not only a woman seeking the truth in the Word of God, but she is also my sister. I've had the privilege of knowing her and her journey my whole life. Having seen her personal walk and experiences first hand, I can guarantee that you are getting the most authentic and real experience she can offer you. Called to Truth is birthed from her journey of learning and growing in the truth of God's word. Through the mountaintops and valleys, she has been taught by the LORD. Her book is packed full of help, hope, and tools for anyone who chooses to follow the ways of our loving Savior Jesus Christ. You will be challenged as you read this book, to believe the word of God and find His power in doing so. This book is for those who are looking for more than the world has to offer. If you are ready to know the One who created you, this book delivers His truth. You were meant to thrive in life, not just survive. This book will show you how to live as an overcomer, thriving in the abundant life Christ died to give you. Be prepared to partake upon the banqueting feast that is set before you as you apply the truth within these pages. It is ultimately your choice to taste and see that the LORD is good. — Paula Wade, Minister of the Gospel of Jesus Christ, Graduate of Charis Bible College

What a great book! I really appreciate all the scripture which is clearly the base of this book, such a great tool. The truth that speaks directly from these pages is life changing from the challenges given in the word of God. Denise's life stories warm my heart and make the book very personable. This is the kind of book when read again and again will speak in a new way. That's the beauty of reading God's word and hearing the truth - it brings clarity of mind. — Tamela Sargent, Former Women's Ministry Leader, Arizona

I have read your book twice and want to thank you for your obedience in writing it. It is in my humble opinion a must-read book for new believers. It answers many of the questions new believers have regarding the Kingdom of God and how it operates. Your testimony, documented experiences, and how you support your experiences with scripture make these lessons easily relatable. Also, I think this book is timely as many are not hearing these principles. This book has been a blessing to me and will bless the body of Christ. — Scott Warnes, born again, spirit-filled believer; Indiana

I would highly recommend reading this book and allowing God to use it as a biblical resource to help powerfully guide you into spiritual wholeness! This anointed resource is saturated with scripture, the Living Word of God! During my friendship with Denise, I have been greatly impacted by her godly character, humility, and hunger for the Truth, which is Jesus Christ! I see a desperate hunger in her to passionately pursue the One True God and to see Jesus Christ set the captives free (Isaiah 61:1-3 and Luke 4:18-19)! She shares her personal testimony and journey with God in a very transparent, personal, and impacting way. The Holy Spirit has led her every step of the way in this powerful journey of discovering, knowing Jesus Christ personally, and learning how to live an overcoming life in God! Called to Truth is a solid, biblical resource and such an amazing gift for the body of Christ to enter into the fullness of what God has for them! Get ready to experience the presence of God and to ask the Holy Spirit to speak, heal, and transform you, because HE will! — Elizabeth Kletti- wholehearted disciple of Jesus Christ

This book is a treasure to have in your hands! Denise encourages you with insightful truths from God's word- the Bible. Her testimony throughout the book shows God's powerful work in her life. She gives tools to live a victorious life in Jesus, by closely examining

your mind, body, and soul. Whether you are a new believer or have known Jesus Christ for some time, you will gain truths and principles to defeat the enemy and live a life God has for you. — Cheryl Fleger, Arizona

Called to Truth

A Practical, Biblical Guide to Spiritual
and Physical Wholeness

DENISE WHITE

Published by KHARIS PUBLISHING, imprint of KHARIS MEDIA LLC.

Copyright © 2020 Denise White

ISBN-13: 978-1-946277-56-5
ISBN-10: 1-946277-56-8

All rights reserved. This book or parts thereof may not be reproduced in any form, stored in a retrieval system, or transmitted in any form by any means - electronic, mechanical, photocopy, recording, or otherwise - without prior written permission of the publisher, except as provided by United States of America copyright law.

All KHARIS PUBLISHING products are available at special quantity discounts for bulk purchase for sales promotions, premiums, fund-raising, and educational needs. For details, contact:

Kharis Media LLC
Tel: 1-479-599-8657
support@kharispublishing.com
www.kharispublishing.com

ACKNOWLEDGEMENT

First and foremost, I praise God for His faithfulness. God has been my strength, my fortress, and my deliverer. I take refuge in Him. He has taken me on this truth-journey that has changed my life forever and has brought me to a place of peace.

I thank God for my husband, Jim. Jim has faithfully provided for our family for the past 31 years, and this has afforded me the opportunity to pursue the dreams God has put on my heart. Thank you, Jim, for your support and love all these years. Thanks for encouraging me to not give up on my dreams.

MY BELIEFS

I believe the Bible is the Word of God and the power and authority for believers. I believe in God the Father. I believe in Jesus Christ as my LORD and Savior, and He is the Son of God. He lived a sinless life on earth and died on the cross for the sins of the world. He rose from the dead. He conquered sin, death, disease, and Satan. Through Jesus Christ's completed work on the cross, we are saved, healed, delivered, preserved, and made whole. I believe in the Holy Spirit. As a disciple of Jesus Christ, I walk by faith not by sight! By the power of the Holy Spirit, I walk in victory and overcome! *"And they overcame him (Satan) by the blood of the Lamb, and by the word of their testimony; and they loved not their lives to the death."* (Revelation 12:11)

MY PURPOSE AND HOPE

This is the testimony of my journey to the truth. My heart's desire is for new truth from the Word of God to be revealed to you, and that you walk out the calling God has for your life. May you have revelation from the Word of God, and may the words of my testimony encourage you in your faith journey.

Each of us, as believers, will be asked to do kingdom work for the LORD. The plans God has for your life will be unique to you. May you be obedient to God and step out boldly for the LORD.

Contact information: dwhite.calledtotruth@gmail.com

DISCLAIMER

This book is not intended to provide medical advice or professional counseling. This book is not intended to take the place of medical treatment or professional counseling. Always consult with your medical health care provider or professional counselor before making any change in your physical regimen regarding fasting, medication, diet, or any treatment. This book is not a substitute for medical care, advice, diagnosis, treatment, or professional counseling

CONTENTS

1	Called to Truth	1
2	My Transformation	4
3	Shining the Light on Lies	7
4	Battle Plan	11
5	The Author of Order	14
6	Our Obedience	26
7	True Identity or Stolen Identity	32
8	Bringing Heaven to Earth (Prayer)	35
9	Our Superpower: The Power of Faith	43
10	Our Guide	48
11	Satan and His Evil Kingdom	55
12	Don't Be Deceived	64
13	Spiritual Roots	69
14	Our Spiritual Authority Through Jesus Christ	72

15	Spiritual Warfare	82
16	Spiritual Check-up	86
17	We Choose	92
18	God's Hospital: Healing, Deliverance, and Wholeness	97
19	Laying On Of Hands	117
20	Relationships Built on Solid Ground	120
21	Truth Changes Fact	126
	Bibliography	129

CHAPTER 1
Called to Truth

Jesus is the Way, the Truth, and the Life., and John 1:11 states that Jesus's own people received Him not. Therefore, in not receiving Jesus, they denied the Truth. Is it easier sometimes to believe lies? The truth will stretch our thinking and cause growing pains, but ultimately it brings us the freedom that our soul longs for. Lies, on the other hand, keep us comfortable and secure for a while but eventually lies catch up with us. Is it easier to numb the mind and feed the flesh with worldly indulgence than it is to challenge oneself with God's truth? God stretches our thinking and causes us to humble our way of thinking, to embrace His ways. God's ways continually grow us to be more like Him. His desire is for us to have the abundant life.

I was hungry for the truth. Mercifully, God showed me how my way of thinking had led me into defeat and frustration. Trying to solve problems, with worldly knowledge, left me dismayed and discouraged. God's word says "to be strong and courageous". Why was I feeling so buried alive with despair? I had made mistakes because of my lack of knowledge and disobedience. I was buried alive with despair because there was a mountain in my life. At the time, I had no revelation of how God had given me tools of spiritual truths to move my mountain. The tools that I was using were the resources of the world and my efforts. The tools of the world were not moving my mountain but keeping me in bondage to those mountains. My journey to truth began when I surrendered my life and my way of thinking to His, and I wanted Him to show me the way to freedom.

Called to Truth

About 15 years ago, my husband and I vacationed at Maui. One of the activities we chose to experience was ziplining. I knew little about ziplining but knew it would move me out of my comfort and challenge me. We began our zipline adventure by putting on our hard hats and harness and then our guide led the way. The first zipline was very short and close to the ground. There were about eight ziplines that gradually increased in length and height. By the time, we arrived at the last zipline, I had built my confidence from this new experience. The last zipline was about 300 feet over a deep gorge, and I overcame my giant that day! I compare this to the journey God has taken me on of "Called to Truth". He moved me from one truth to another and showed me how to overcome. Come along with me as I take you on a zipline adventure of truth and overcoming! The more truth that was penetrating my being, the more I searched for answers and a deeper understanding. *"For the Word of God is quick, and powerful, and sharper than any two-edged sword, piercing even to the dividing asunder of soul and spirit, and of the joints and marrow, and is a discerner of the thoughts and intents of the heart"* (Hebrews 4:12). The truth of God reveals His amazing power. When His power is revealed to us, it frees us from bondage.

Part of my search for truth began with Mark 16:15-20, John 14:12, and Revelation 10:11. I knew God's word was true, so why was I not seeing evidence of Mark 16 in my life. According to Mark 16:15-20, **those who believe** are to cast out demons; speak in new tongues; remove Satan from their lives (take up serpents); anything we drink (receive into our soul) will not hurt us; and lay hands on the sick and they will recover. Additionally in John 14:12, **Jesus said those who believe would do what He did, and we would do greater works when He ascended to go to the Father**. Why was I not seeing this? What truth did I not yet know or understand? Where are the believers who have faith for these things? I wanted to be one of those that believe!! Revelation 10:11 says we are to overcome Satan in our own lives and have a testimony. I wanted my testimony. After asking, seeking, and knocking, spiritual truths were revealed to me.

There is so much more to your story of transformation once you accept Jesus as your LORD and Savior. He has work for you to do. He has truth He wants you to learn so you can help others learn of His saving grace and be set free. After salvation, it is a lie if you think everything in your life will be easier. It is just the beginning of the good fight of faith. Life with Jesus Christ brings freedom, but it is a battle to keep Satan and the world from stealing that freedom. Once you have a personal revelation of God's truth in your own life, your heart's desire will be to help others know the same freedom. The Word of God never says the faith walk is easy, but the rewards are immeasurable which include eternal life.

What does freedom through Jesus Christ mean to me? It means that I have accepted Jesus Christ as my LORD and Savior. It means I can talk to

God any time, and I am never alone. It means the Holy Spirit is my Guide. He will lead me into living a life of obedience. It means I no longer agree with fear because it comes from Satan, the father of lies. It means I know that I am commanded by God to love myself, and I will not let Satan tell me otherwise. It means I fear God and want to please God, not man. It means that Jesus Christ defeated Satan. Through Jesus Christ, I am saved, healed, delivered, preserved, and made whole. It means the Word of God, God the Father, God the Son, and God the Holy Spirit are the only places that I will find complete and absolute truth. Truth is freedom!

    I pray that whatever the LORD wants to reveal to you this book will be a catalyst for change in your life. The Word of God will transform your life. I don't want you to miss out on God's best for your life; fight for the abundant life.

CHAPTER 2

My Transformation

I was ready for a change! I was tired of striving with futile efforts and still having a heavy burden. My efforts were not producing peaceful results, but instead, continual turmoil that seemed to have no end. *"Therefore if any man be in Christ, he is a new creature: old things are passed away; behold, all things are become new"* (2 Corinthians 5:17). When we let Jesus Christ into our heart, He transforms us. When our minds are renewed, according to Romans 12:2, we are transformed. When Jesus transforms our hearts and minds, we are a new creation. I needed to choose to turn my life over to Jesus, and I finally came to a place where I understood what that meant. I came to a place of humility and surrender.

My journey with the LORD began at a very young age. My loving mother was faithful in taking me to church and Sunday school as a little girl. I loved the LORD as far back as I can remember. Yet when I was young I didn't understand the relationship He wanted with me. Now I have a personal testimony of my relationship with Jesus Christ and how He has set me free. Through the trials of life, I was moved to seek truth because of my overwhelming feeling of confusion and dismay. I knew I had to get out of my comfort zone and out of my current thinking patterns, to see what God wanted to reveal to me. I desired to go on a spiritual journey with the LORD.

I told God that I wanted to go on a journey with Him to deepen our relationship and deepen my knowledge and wisdom. Life had become extremely difficult and my inner man (soul) wouldn't rest until it knew the truth. The Holy Spirit led me through a journey of many revelations. I had a lot of questions like "why do many believers seem defeated?," "why are there so many 'unbelieving' believers?," "the Bible says believers are to overcome, but what are we to overcome?" One of the most important things about this time was that I couldn't put boundaries on God, and His revelations to me. I wanted to seek the truth in any way God wanted to reveal it to me. Setting boundaries on God and His truth is very dangerous because we have to trust Him, and His truth should be our ultimate desire. When we have revelation, the Word of God becomes real to us, and it changes who we are on the inside. It is not just words printed on a page, but it is alive and breathes life and freedom into believers.

I was baptized as an infant. Later in life, as I grew in the knowledge of the truth, I came to understand the importance of baptism by immersion. The word baptism in Greek and Hebrew means to immerse. Mark 16:16 says, *"He that believes and is baptized shall be saved . . ."* These truths led me to be baptized in 2008. Continuing in my spiritual growth, I visited a healing room in 2014. They laid hands on me to receive the baptism of the Holy Spirit, and I received the gift of speaking in tongues. I was baptized a second time, in 2017, as new truths were revealed to me, and I wanted to confess my sin of fear and rebuke it that very day. These were important days in my spiritual walk as I grew to understand how God's truth and power brought me freedom.

As new truths transformed my heart, my life was transformed. I was a very quiet child and had a lot of fear. I wasn't even aware of the extent of my fears until I matured. Looking back on my younger self I would say fear held me captive. As I became older and wiser, I made some life choices that pushed me out of my comfort zone and fear fled, but my inner being (soul) was wounded from the fear I had agreed with. I didn't even know I had a choice to say "no" to fear and to walk into a life of freedom and faith. I felt like a prisoner in my own body because I felt like I wasn't who God created me to be. I wasn't created to be silent or afraid. As I grew in my spiritual walk and spent more time in the Word of God, the life-giving power of the Word of God transformed me. You can read scripture and intellectually understand the words; but when you hear and meditate on the Word of God and it penetrates your heart and mind, you become a new creation. The Word of God says I am made in His image and I am fearfully and wonderfully made, and I now believe this in my soul. I know my worth to the Creator! I now agree with what God says about me, not the lies in my head. God has prepared work for me to do, and I don't want to miss out on His plans for my life. Ephesians 2:10, *"for we are His workmanship, created in Christ Jesus to good works, which God has before ordained that we should walk in them.*" If I continue to walk in the lies in my head that say "I can't do that" or "I am not intelligent enough" or "they do a better job than I could do" then I miss out on what God is leading me to do. When I walk into the plans God has prepared for me, I am right where He wants me to be.

My spiritual journey of allowing the truth to penetrate my mind and transform me included studying the Bible; prayer and quiet time with the LORD; listening and studying pastors' sermons; seeking the truth from spirit-filled and full gospel churches and various ministries; visiting healing and deliverance ministries for truth; reading books on faith, healing and deliverance; listening to YouTube teachings on Prophetic Dreams, Gifts of the Spirit, Healing and Deliverance; and studying and discussing God's word with fellow believers. During this time, I was also in two different Bible studies. Additionally, my sister, Paula, has been my spiritual mentor/teacher for a long time, and we spoke often over the telephone about what God was teaching us during the week. These were my intentional steps in seeking the LORD. When you earnestly seek the LORD, He will reveal Himself to you. When you keep seeking and asking God to direct your steps, He will!

During this season of seeking answers from the LORD, I went to ministry conferences and healing and deliverance ministries. This was eye-opening to see how God was working in different ways; ways that I had never personally known. When I went to a healing room they laid hands on me, anointed me with oil, and prayed over me. Two ministry people laid hands on me to receive the baptism of the Holy Spirit. I spoke in tongues that day. "*For he who speaks in a tongue does not speak to men but to God, for no one understands him; however, in the spirit he speaks mysteries*" (1 Corinthians 14:2).

This truth journey has taught me how to use my discernment in seeking God's truth. I trusted that God was leading me on this journey. This was a very intentional period of growing in God's knowledge and wisdom. I did not let fear stop me on this journey. Satan kept trying to make me fear that I was going to learn the wrong teachings. The LORD led me, and I trusted Him on this journey. I knew His truth would prevail. This spiritual growth has been the most life-changing period of my life.

When God takes you on a very personal journey of spiritual growth, you are never the same again. The growth we experience when we allow God to direct our steps is completely transforming. Being a Christian my whole life, I had never examined my beliefs or tried to look outside of my comfort level to see what God wanted to show me. I needed to become a participant in my spiritual growth, not just receive what someone else said. I needed to practice my discernment and be able to distinguish good from evil, and truth from a lie. I needed to learn how to wait on the Holy Spirit for revelation. This is my journey of transformation . . .

CHAPTER 3

Shining the Light on Lies

When God shined the light on the lies in my life, I recognized fear was the biggest liar. I realized I was serving fear. *"For God hath not given us the spirit of fear; but of power, and of love, and of a sound mind"* (2 Timothy 1:7). Therefore, God didn't give me fear. Who gave me fear? Satan did. Without realizing it, I had agreed with fear and was serving fear. Lies chain us to the darkness and God's truth draws and connects us to the light. The beliefs of the world and Satan's schemes will try to fight for our attention and try to steal God's truth from us. My soul had such a yearning for truth. I didn't understand what it meant to be an overcomer since I really didn't see people overcoming; and where was the abundant life spoken about in the Bible? I knew I was missing something. I wanted answers to some very deep spiritual questions. When struggles lead us to seek God's truth for answers, we are more willing to hear what God has to say. I had to put aside the belief systems that were built into me over the years of incorrect thinking patterns. One of the most important things when seeking the LORD is humility. If we come with pride, we won't hear the truth because we think we already know the truth. My mind, heart, and free will were wide open to the mysteries God wanted to reveal to me.

I had to accept that I had believed some things that were lies. When you believe a lie, you don't know it is a lie, but Satan has deceived you. An analogy would be when you unknowingly open an email that has a virus. An infected email contains malicious code and can bring a virus into your email and computer. It causes problems for you, and it intends to harm your computer system. But once you know the signs to look for in an infected email, you are more aware and can take precautionary measures. Just like when you become aware that Satan is trying to deceive you, and you learn to guard against his lies and schemes. The Holy Spirit taught me discernment which enabled me to recognize good from evil. Never let fear lead you in your search for the truth. Fear will rob you of knowing the truth! Fear is Satan's way of keeping you from the truth.

According to 2 Corinthians 3:18, *"But we all, with open face beholding as in a glass the glory of the LORD, are changed into the same image from glory to glory, even as by the Spirit of the LORD."* The truth changes us when we follow the truth in obedience. The more of God's truth that is revealed to us, the more life-giving this is to our body, mind, and soul. When I am studying a scripture verse, I will check various translations for clarification; I will listen for the Holy Spirit to lead me to understand; I will meditate on a particular scripture in the King James Version; I will read the definition in Hebrew or Greek; and I will study the Strong's Concordance for that verse. These are all very helpful when meditating on scripture. We need to seek for ourselves the Word of God and allow the Holy Spirit to lead us. I also had to align my thoughts with the Word of God. Part of my spiritual journey was evaluating my current belief system. I asked myself "where did I learn that from" and just because I believed something for years doesn't mean it is true. The truth is I was deceived and I needed to embrace the truth and discard the lies.

Deception and lies can come from various forms:
1) It can come from a statement someone made about you that was a lie, and you agreed with it.
2) It could come from Satan and his evil kingdom.
3) It could be a false teaching you heard and believed.
4) It could be a lie that began in your thoughts, and you agreed with it and ruminated on the lie.
5) It could be a lie you learned from the world.
6) It could be an incorrect thinking pattern you grew up believing.
7) It could come from your false understanding of what a word means and a lie develops from that.
8) It could be from ignorance.

9) It could be from traditions you learned and accepted as truth.
10) It could come from accepting a partial truth. A partial truth can be deceptive because there is some truth but a falsehood is included; therefore, it is a lie.
11) It could come from disqualifying parts of the Bible that you weren't comfortable with. In that way, you can become an unbeliever of parts of scripture.

These are just some of the ways I have learned lies develop. Lies, ultimately, are all from Satan's evil kingdom. The reason for finding out where the lie has come from is to be aware of the entrance point of the lie, to then prevent it from happening again. You must develop an awareness of how Satan deceives you.

These lies can build and cause you to have doubt instead of faith. I have included a large amount of scripture to assist you in your truth-seeking. Pray that God reveals to you any lies that you currently believe. The LORD moves us from glory to glory as we follow His truth.

The world's truth and man's truth are up for interpretation. The world's truth changes over time. Man's truth is affected by our personal experiences and thought patterns. Much of the evening news is debating what is true and who do you believe. Now with the term "fake news" or "junk news" becoming so prevalent, people don't know what is misinformation, hoaxes, sensationalism, or dishonest. Right and wrong, truth and lies are becoming very muddled in the news. The Word of God never changes and is the same yesterday, today, and tomorrow. The only thing that does not change is God and His word.

God's word says that some people keep learning but never know the truth! *"Ever learning, and never able to come to the knowledge of the truth"* (2 Timothy 3:7). When we meditate on God's word and let the Holy Spirit guide us into truth, God will bring clarity and new revelation to us. When we earnestly seek Him, He rewards us. Truths that are revealed to us will always agree with the Word of God, God the Father, God the Son (Jesus Christ), and God the Holy Spirit. Thereby, we will be able to test what we are learning and come to the knowledge of the Truth.

I knew, in my spirit, I was to seek until I found answers to my questions. I would read in scripture how we are more than conquerors, but I didn't see that in my life or others around me. I knew I was missing something that God wanted to reveal to me. How could I help myself or anyone else if I didn't know the truth? A lie will not set anyone free. God led me on several journeys into truth where He took me to a special location where my time was fully devoted to Him. I was enlisted in "truth basic training" and the Holy Spirit was my Guide. As you keep seeking truth, lies won't have anywhere to live, and they will lose their hold on you.

In the early stages of writing my journey of truth, God gave me two separate words. The first word He gave me was "compass" and the second was "Titanic". As I sought the LORD asking him what this meant, it was revealed to me that I would bring order to situations, that were sinking, when I followed the truth.

My journey into truth Bible verses are:
"The Spirit of truth, whom the world cannot receive, because it neither sees Him nor knows Him; but you know Him, for He dwells with you and will be in you" (John 14:17).

"My people are destroyed for lack of knowledge. . . ." (Hosea 4:6).

"And you shall know the truth, and the truth shall make you free. . ." (John 8:32)

"For the weapons of our warfare are not carnal, but mighty through God to pulling down of strongholds; casting down imaginations, and every high thing that exalts itself against the knowledge of God, bringing into captivity every thought to the obedience of Christ" (2 Corinthians 10:4-5).

"For the wisdom of this world is foolishness with God. For it is written, He taketh the wise in their own craftiness" (1 Corinthians 3:19).

"However, when He, the Spirit of truth, has come, He will guide you into all truth . . ." (John 16:13-14).

"Let not mercy and truth forsake thee: bind them about my neck; write them upon the table of thine heart" (Proverbs 3:3).

"The LORD is near to all them that call upon Him, to all that call upon Him in truth" (Psalm 145:18).

CHAPTER 4

Battle Plan

One afternoon a friend and I prayed for a young man's salvation. I don't have words to explain the power that we felt in our prayer that day. Shortly after we prayed, this person had a series of traumatic events occur in his life. It began with a government authority claiming a financial obligation was due. A short time later, this person's health was under major attack with emergency room visits weekly, at times even daily. During this time, this person was working on an incredible medical breakthrough that would have amazing implications when completed. This person was the only one who had the experience and knowledge to complete the research at this level of expertise. Due to the person's severe health problems, the research had to be put on hold. During all of this upheaval, I found out this person was having very disturbing demonic dreams frequently. I don't exactly know how our prayers affected any of these events, but I know that our prayer did have significant implications in the spiritual realm. I don't think I understood the level of spiritual warfare for people's souls. This story, along with other events, escalated my desire to seek God for answers and truth about the spirit realm. I needed to understand.

When you are facing a trial or difficulty, how do you approach the situation? As a believer in the LORD Jesus Christ, we need to approach our situation with a spiritual mindset. When we involve God in our problems, He will work things out for our good as we follow His direction.

We are soldiers fighting real battles, and as Christ-followers, we should have our battle plan ready. What is your battle plan when trouble strikes? What if you could prevent some of your struggles from even happening because you knew God's order and His commands and followed them. If you were missing some truths from scripture that would help you lead a more abundant life, wouldn't you want to know what they were? Once I had a new revelation of God's truth, I wanted to help others be prepared so when a difficulty came their way, they would be armed and ready for battle in the spirit realm.

When you are a soldier in a battle, you need to know the instructions of your commanding officer. Do you know the truth God has given us so that you can live a more abundant life? Are you using the spiritual authority God has given you as a believer? Do you know what God's instructions (Word of God) are telling you? Do you spend time learning God's truths from His word or is your time spent on the world's knowledge?

"A battle plan sets forth methods for the coordinated employment of forces during the battle." If you are using the wrong methods to battle your storm, for instance, if you have been taught a lie and don't know God's truth, your plans to defeat Satan may fail. When your boots are on the ground fighting a spiritual battle, you need to know the truth from the Word of God, put on the full armor of God, and have your battle plan ready to defeat the enemy.

A soldier needs to know his enemy and their tactics. Satan is the father of lies and the accuser of our brethren. Don't allow Satan to use you as his mouthpiece here on earth speaking lies and accusing your brethren. After Jesus was baptized, He fasted for 40 days and nights. During this time, Satan appeared to Jesus and tried to tempt Him. Satan left Jesus after He refused the temptations. Jesus knew scripture and how to rebuke Satan. We also need to be prepared with the Word of God to rebuke Satan (John 8:44, Revelation 12:9-11).

According to John 10:10, *"The thief cometh not, but for to steal, and to kill, and to destroy: I am come that they might have life, and that they might have it more abundantly."* If we know how to protect our homes from thieves, shouldn't we know how to spiritually protect ourselves and our families from the thief (Satan)? It is easy to forget that the spiritual battle between the kingdom of darkness and the Kingdom of Light is continually going on in the spirit realm when you can't see it in the physical realm. Unless you learn to fight the battle God's way, you can become defeated. When you are a warrior for the LORD, you need to fight with God's word and put on the whole armor of God. See Ephesians 6:11-18.

As I was learning to walk in new truths, my decisions and decision-making process changed. I think I was on automatic pilot when it came to problem-solving. I immediately would try to solve problems with my worldly knowledge and resources. I didn't understand that God wanted to be involved in all aspects of my life and had the ultimate answer to all of my problems. My problem-solving techniques were only patching the problem up temporarily. I was becoming exhausted, frustrated, and discouraged. I didn't quite understand the difference between striving God's way versus striving the world's way. God didn't want me to sit back and do nothing, but He wanted me to ask Him how to proceed. The other major part of my journey to discovery was to understand that I was in a spiritual battle. I was looking at everything from the world's view and not the spiritual aspect. I didn't have any understanding of spiritual warfare or my spiritual authority. I did not understand that I was searching the world for answers: where the answers couldn't be found. The world would never give my soul peace for the questions I had. But God would unveil to me the truths of His word that washes away the confusion of the world. When I looked for answers in all the wrong places, I came up empty. The Holy Spirit led me to areas where I would uncover His truth. The searching I needed to do was going to be in the spiritual, not the natural.

CHAPTER 5

The Author of Order

God is slowly being removed from our government, our schools, the family unit, and individual lives. The more that God is removed from our lives, the more disorder that ensues. Prayer has been taken out of most schools. Today, school shootings are not uncommon. The Ten Commandment monuments have been taken down from government buildings. In the name of women's rights and pro-choice, millions of babies have been murdered through abortion. According to a National Right to Life report, since Roe v. Wade in 1973, there have been 60,942,033 abortions. God created the family, but the world is redefining "family" according to what culture says is acceptable. God is the author of order, and Satan, sin, and the world are the authors of chaos.

The Word of God says we are to hate sin and evil. God defines sin and evil, not man. In the name of tolerance, we tolerate things in our world that God never said His children were to tolerate. God's laws and commands are to protect us from evil. When we remove God's laws and commands from our nation, His protection is removed. Chaos will ensue as more and more "tolerance" continues. In the name of tolerance, it appears we agree with evil. When we submit to evil, we give evil access to our lives.

God's order can be found in His commandments, His wisdom and knowledge, the Word of God, and the Godhead (Father, Son, and Holy

Spirit). Disorder is found in lawlessness, the world system, Satan and his evil kingdom, and our disobedience to God.

In Genesis 18-19, there was grievous sinning among the people of Sodom and Gomorrah. God said He would not destroy the city of Sodom if he could find ten righteous men. God could not find ten righteous men! God was going to destroy the city because of their iniquity. God rained brimstone and fire out of heaven onto Sodom and Gomorrah, and Lot and his wife were told not to look back as they ran to escape. As Lot and his wife were escaping Sodom, Lot's wife looked back at Sodom and became a pillar of salt. The people of Sodom and Gomorrah were lawless and disobedient. What does God see on the earth today? What are God's children doing for the Kingdom of God? As followers of Jesus Christ, we are to bring light into the darkness. We are to turn from evil and not look back. We are in a spiritual battle to bring God's order to earth. As His followers, we need to agree with God and bring heaven to earth.

OUR RELATIONSHIP WITH GOD

We can't let the world and its distractions take us away from our first love, the LORD. The LORD intended us to have an intimate relationship with Him. When we have a personal relationship with our LORD, we will have the fullness He offers. Abundant life, in Jesus, is living with a renewed mind and pure heart. Then we can live above our circumstances as we battle evil and overcome the forces of deception in our lives.

In the Book of Daniel, Daniel was taken captive by Nebuchadnezzar at about 14 or 15 years of age. He was taken to Babylon where they worshipped many gods. Daniel was a Jewish boy who grew up loving and worshipping God. He was taken away from everything he knew, but he stayed faithful to God regardless of his circumstances. Daniel rose in power in Babylon as the king trusted Daniel. Daniel interpreted dreams for the king. Regardless of Daniel rising in power under the king, Daniel's priority was his relationship with God. Daniel would go into his house and pray three times a day to God. Later during King Darius's reign, he made a decree that no one was to pray to anyone but him. Daniel continued praying to God, three times a day, regardless of the king's decree. King Darius put Daniel in the lions' den for praying to God. But God sent His angel and shut the lions' mouth. Daniel kept obeying God and God was faithful to take care of Him. Daniel's relationship with God was the most important thing for Daniel. Throughout Daniel's captivity, he had many temptations, but he was found faithful. As followers of Jesus, this world is our foreign land. Daniel kept praying to God regardless of who told him to stop and regardless of his other responsibilities.

When the LORD returns one day as the Judge, how many will He find faithful?

GODLY ORDER

God's order is His law which is the Word of God. God and His word never change. In Exodus 20, He gave us the Ten Commandments which are as true today as they were then. In Matthew 22:37-40, *"Jesus said unto him, Thou shalt love the LORD thy God with all thy heart, and with all thy soul, and with all thy mind. This is the first and great commandment. And the second is like unto it, Thou shalt love thy neighbor as thyself. <u>On these two commandments hang all the law and the prophets</u>."* Our LORD never changes, and His truth never changes. *"Jesus Christ is the same yesterday, and today, and forever"* (Hebrews 13:8).

God's order includes order within the Godhead. God has placed Jesus at His right hand in the heavenly places far above all principalities, powers, rulers of the darkness of this world,, and spiritual wickedness in high places. The name of Jesus is above all names. God has order within the Godhead; God the Father, God the Son, and God the Holy Spirit. The following scripture verses can be studied to further understand the Godhead (2 Corinthians 3:17, 2 Corinthians 13:14, Colossians 2:9, Isaiah 9:6, John 10:30, Matthew 28:19, John 5:19).

Order is of God; confusion is of Satan. *"Woe to the rebellious children, saith the LORD, that take counsel, but not of Me; and that cover with a covering, but not of My Spirit, that they may add sin to sin"* (Isaiah 30:1). God is our covering and protection, and we are accountable to God. If we are only relying on an earthly spiritual leader to hear the Word of God and are not studying the Word of God on our own, we can be led astray into false teaching or false understanding. We need to be able to spiritually discern good from evil for ourselves. We need to allow the Holy Spirit to lead us in our spiritual growth and truth. God will draw us to Him and His truth which keeps us from being deceived.

All men are under the order and authority God has set up. According to Romans 13:1, *"Let every soul be subject unto the higher powers. For there is no power but of God: the powers that be are ordained by God."* Whether you are the person in authority or the person under the authority, you are responsible to God for your actions. He sees all things and knows all things. God does not tolerate rebellion on either side. This may seem obvious, but if you look at the world, we are in a lot of rebellion. One example of this is the family. God created the family, and we are rebelling as a nation by redefining the family (1 Samuel 15:23, Ephesians 5:21-25).

God has a plan and purpose for each person's life. God made each of us wonderfully in our mother's womb. *"For you formed my inward parts; You covered* me in my mother's womb. I will praise You, for I am fearfully and wonderfully made; Marvelous are Your works, and that my soul knows very well. My frame was not hidden from You, When I was made in secret, And skillfully wrought in the lowest parts of the earth. Your eyes saw my substance, being yet unformed. And in Your book they all were written, The days fashioned for me, When as yet there were none of them" (Psalm 139:13-16). As you read the entire chapter of Psalm 139, you will find that the LORD loves you so much that He knows your behavior and patterns. He lovingly watches you. He knows more about you than anyone else.

God not only has order within the Godhead but an order within the family. *"But I would have you know, that the head of every man is Christ; and the head of the woman is the man; and the head of Christ is God"* (1 Corinthians 11:3). God created marriage between a man and a woman. God has placed the husband as the head of the family. Within the family, wives are to submit to their husbands. The husband is the head of the wife as Christ is head of the Church. Husbands are to love their wives as Christ loves the Church. Furthermore, children are to honor and obey their parents. When our homes follow God's order, the family will be in peace, not strife. Our obedience to God's design will bring blessings to our family (Colossians 3:18-22, Ephesians 5:31-33).

Marriage is sacred to God and was instituted by God in the book of Genesis. *"Therefore shall a man leave his father and his mother, and shall cleave unto his wife: and they shall be one flesh"* (Genesis 2:24). Marriage is a covenant created by God between a man and a woman.

God desires His people to dwell in unity. *"Behold how good and pleasant it is for brethren to dwell together in unity"* (Psalm 133:1). God wants the husband and wife unified. God wants the family united. God wants us to unify in prayer with other believers. When we agree, there is much power (Matthew 18:19).

When we follow God's order, we are coming into agreement with His plans for our life. If we disagree with God's order, we are in rebellion and opening the door to evil.

GOD'S AUTHORITY

According to 2 Timothy 2:1-4, believers are chosen as the LORD's soldiers, and we are assigned to the LORD's work as He commissions us in Mark 16:15-20. We are to submit to God and reign under His authority. We are to be wise in the understanding of God's kingdom and be willing to be foolish in the eyes of the world.

God has authority over all principalities and powers of light and darkness. God has given His disciples the Keys of the Kingdom. When someone gives you their house keys, you have access to what is in their home. When we use the Keys of the Kingdom and reign under God's authority, we will see people set free and bring heaven to earth (Colossians 2:9-10, Romans 5:17).

THE WORD OF GOD

God's will is His word. Seek the Word of God to find out the will of God. We will know the will of God from the Word of God, from the commandments in the Bible, from the covenants and promises in the Bible, and through the Holy Spirit. God is a covenant-keeping God. God does not go against His covenant or His Word (Hebrews 10:36).

The Word of God will reveal to us when something is wrong in our soul. The Word of God is our discerner. God's word has supernatural power to penetrate the soul and spirit, and joints and marrow. According to Hebrews 4:12, *"For the Word of God is quick, and powerful, and sharper than any two edged sword, piercing even to the dividing asunder of soul and spirit, and of the joints and marrow, and is a discerner of the thoughts and intents of the heart."*

We are not only called to hear the Word of God but to be doers of the Word of God. We are either in the camp of God, where we are walking in obedience or the camp of Satan. We are either submitting to God, or we are not (James 1:22).

Finally, are we seeking to be biblically correct or are we seeking to be politically correct? Are we trying to have peace with the world or peace with God?

FEAR OF GOD (types of fear)

What does it mean to fear God? First of all, there are different types of fear. The type of fear that alerts us to danger; for example: if a bear is coming towards us, this fear is a fight or flight response and God intended this for our protection. A type of fear that gives us wisdom, to move in a situation for our benefit, is godly fear. A fear from Satan would be a fear of torment; fear of tomorrow, fear of death, etc. Lastly and most importantly, fear of God is awe, respect, and obedience to the Almighty (2 Timothy 1:7, 1 John 4:18, Deuteronomy 6:24).

<u>Fear of God is acknowledging His authority, standing in awe of Him, and His holiness; and therefore, responding in obedience</u>. We are not to be afraid of God because then we will not have a close intimate relationship with Him or go to Him in need. We need to understand God is love, and He operates out of love for us. Therefore, our loving Father may do things we don't understand, but we need to know He is working out all things for our good. If a loving earthly father wants good for his children, how much more does our Heavenly Father want good for us. A child of God does not know all the

mysteries that God the Father does, but we trust in Him. We fear Him because He knows all things and does all things from the place of love (Deuteronomy 10:12).

SALVATION AND SANCTIFICATION

Jesus Christ is the Son of the living God. The gospel is the good news that Jesus Christ came to earth as a man, died on the cross, paid the price for our sins, resurrected from the dead, ascended into heaven, and will return as the Judge of the earth. When we say we believe in Jesus Christ as our LORD and Savior, this means we trust Him, follow Him, and obey Him. *"For God so loved the world, that He gave His only begotten Son, that whosoever believes in Him should not perish, but have everlasting life"* (John 3:16).

When we believe in the redemptive work of Jesus Christ as the Son of the living God, we will respond by repenting of sin (change our mind); make a confession that Jesus Christ is LORD; obey Him; remain faithful with godly sorrow which works repentance to salvation. *"That if you shall confess with your mouth the LORD Jesus, and shall believe in your heart that God has raised Him from the dead, you shall be saved. For with the heart man believes to righteousness; and with the mouth confession is made to salvation"* (Romans 10:9-10).

Part of our obedience to God is being baptized (immersion). According to Acts 22:16, *"And now why tarriest (delay) you? Arise, and be baptized, and wash away your sins, calling on the name of the LORD."* When we believe in Jesus Christ as our LORD and Savior, we trust Him, follow Him, and obey Him. Being baptized is obeying what God's word says. Mark 16:16 says, *"He that believes and is baptized shall be saved: but he that believes not shall be damned."* Also, I suggest reading Acts 2:38-47 to understand more fully the importance of our obedience and being baptized.

What does it mean to be born again? Being born again is when God imparts eternal life to those who accept Jesus as their Savior and are dead in their sins. "Jesus answered and said to him, *'Verily, verily, I say to you, Except a man be born again, he cannot see the kingdom of God'* " (John 3:3). When you are born again, your spirit is resurrected from the dead. Your life radically changes when you are born again. We are no longer separated from God when we are born again. We are sealed by the Holy Spirit (Ephesians 1:13). When we are born again, the Holy Spirit will make us aware of sin, and we will be guided into truth. A born again Christian believes that Jesus Christ is the Son of God and believes Jesus's redemptive work on the cross is finished (Acts 8:36-38); and is drawn and led by the Holy Spirit (John 14:26), drawn to repentance, and is baptized (Acts 2:38); and godly sorrow works repentance to salvation (2 Corinthians 7:9-10).

Called to Truth

A born again believer:

- o <u>Confesses Christ</u> (Matthew 10:32, Romans 10:9-11).
- o <u>Is drawn and led by the Holy Spirit</u> (John 14:26).
- o <u>Drawn to repentance and baptism</u> (Acts 2:38-41, Acts 22:16, Matthew 28:19, Mark 16:16). Being baptized is part of our obedience. There may be circumstances where baptism is not possible like the thief on the cross (Luke 23:42-43). Being baptized is part of obeying God, and we need to be careful if we are choosing not to be baptized (immersion) because of disobedience. There was a time when I wasn't baptized by immersion, and I would tell myself things to justify not wanting to be baptized (immersion). When we obey God, we will need to step out of our comfort. There is power in baptism, and there is power in our obedience. Being baptized was a part of the process for me, of being set free and born again! According to Romans 6:3-4, baptism by immersion is a representation of dying to our old man when we go down in the water and are raised to new life when we come out of the water in baptism.
- o <u>Has godly sorrow which leads to repentance and salvation</u> (2 Corinthians 7:9-10).
- o My born again experience was a purification process as the Holy Spirit would reveal more truth to me, and I would need to respond in obedience.

An erring born again believer needs to: (as a born again believer, we are not to practice sinning)

- o <u>Repent and pray</u> (Acts 8:21-23). Repent is to change one's mind.
- o <u>Confess sins</u> (1 John 1:9). Confession is to admit or declare yourself guilty.

Through the blood of Jesus, we are overcomers. As a born again believer, we are not to practice sinning. When the Holy Spirit leads us to recognize sin, we are to repent (change one's mind), pray, and confess our sin (sorrowfully acknowledge our sin). We are to stand in faith and proclaim the victory we have over Satan by the power of the blood of Jesus and His victory on the cross. We declare and decree that through the blood of Jesus we are justified (just as if we never sinned) and are sanctified (made holy). Through the blood of Jesus, all my sins are forgiven, and I am redeemed out of the hand of Satan. Through the blood of Jesus, I have the boldness to come before God, and I am seated in heavenly places (Hebrews 10:19).

As believers, we undergo a process of sanctification where we are made holy. The Greek definition of sanctification is making holy, set apart, holiness. Acts 26:18 explains sanctification, *"to open their (spiritual) eyes so that they may turn from darkness to light and from the power of Satan to God, that they may receive forgiveness and release from their sins and an inheritance among those who have been sanctified (set apart, made holy) by faith in Me."* Through sanctification, we see through our spiritual eyes the truth, and we will have a great hate for sin and will run to the light of Jesus Christ.

TRIALS AND TEMPTATIONS

What is the purpose of the trials we have in life, and why are we tempted? God's people are tested to show their heart and thoughts. *"The refining pot is for silver and the furnace for gold, But the LORD tests the hearts"* (Proverbs 17:3). Metal is tested for purity, and our hearts are tested by God for purity. What is in our hearts will be revealed when we are tested.

To be able to do God's kingdom work, our faith needs to be refined. We are saved through faith, and we do all God's kingdom work in faith, to bring His kingdom to earth. Through the trials of life, our faith is tested. While we are being refined in these tests, the impurities of unbelief are removed. *"Strengthening and establishing the hearts of the disciples; encouraging them to remain firm in the faith, saying, 'It is through many tribulations and hardships that we must enter the kingdom of God"* (Acts 14:22).

Satan harasses mankind by tempting them to do evil and to destroy the work of God. *"Fear none of those things which thou shalt suffer: behold, the devil shall cast some of you into prison, that ye may be tried; and ye shall have tribulation ten days: be thou faithful unto death, and I will give thee a crown of life"* (Revelation 2:10). Satan is the accuser, the father of lies, a counterfeit, a deceiver, and a master manipulator. God wants His sons and daughters to recognize and overcome the lies of Satan.

The way we handle a trial or temptation will either glorify God or open the door to Satan. The LORD wants us to recognize Satan and his traps; therefore, we will avoid opening the door to Satan. When we know God's order and are obedient to God, we will slam the door closed on Satan and his evil kingdom. *"Blessed is the man who endures temptation; for when he has been approved, he will receive the crown of life which the LORD has promised to those who love Him"* (James 1:12).

REPENTANCE

God is gracious and merciful to us, but this does not excuse us from being responsible for our sin and repenting. Revelation 3:19 says, *"As many as I love, I rebuke and chasten: be zealous therefore, and repent."* Once we repent (change of mind) and confess (to acknowledge/admit sin), the LORD will repair what is broken (Hosea 6:1). Once we have had heartfelt repentance for past sin, we do not look back. God has forgiven us, and He no longer remembers (Ezekiel 18:30-32, Psalm 103:12).

FORGIVENESS

The Greek definition of forgiveness is releasing someone from an obligation or debt. It means a pardon. It is a command from God to forgive no matter what the offense. We do not want to disobey God Almighty. We need to forgive our brother and sister from our hearts. James 4:12 states, *"There is one lawgiver, who is able to save and to destroy: who art thou that judgest your neighbor?"* We shouldn't have to consider whether we will forgive others, but it should be an automatic response to forgive because it is commanded by God. We can pray and ask God to help us forgive. We need to release that person to God because God is the Judge.

We need to choose to forgive. Identify if you are bitter towards anyone, determine what they owe you, then cancel the debt, and close the account. We are not only commanded by God to forgive others but to also forgive ourselves (Colossians 3:13).

OBEDIENCE

Believing the LORD is trusting Him, following Him, and obeying Him. Obedience to the LORD is key to following the LORD's will and having His protection over our lives. When we walk in obedience to God, all things are possible (Luke 6:46-49).

We are to fear the LORD by obeying Him and humbling ourselves before Him. When we are obedient to God, we will be blessed. When God gives us direction in our lives, we need to be willing to follow His direction. When we are humble before Him, we will receive His direction and apply it to our lives (Deuteronomy 6:2).

We are to love God above all else, love ourselves, and love men. We are to put God first in our lives and have no other gods before us (placing possessions, people, or things before God; images, idols). We are commanded by God to love ourselves and our brother. First John 3:10 says, *"In this the children of God are manifest, and the children of the devil: whosoever doeth not righteousness is not of God, neither he that loveth not his brother."* Our actions and the condition of our hearts will reveal whether we are children of God.

Part of our obedience is intentionally evaluating our thoughts and removing any evil thoughts. The enemy attacks us in our minds. The mind of sinful man is death. Therefore, we must take captive every thought to be obedient to Christ and cast down imaginations. We need to cast down incorrect thoughts. If Satan gets us to agree with evil thoughts, he will take us down into a trap of destruction (2 Corinthians 10:5, Romans 8:6).

Fear of the LORD will lead us to obedience. When we are disobedient to God, we are agreeing with Satan and his lies. We are either submitting to God or Satan. Our disobedience leads us into bondage, and we then miss the freedom Jesus wants us to have. Our submission to the Holy Spirit will lead us into the truth and direct our steps into obedience. The power of the Holy Spirit gives us the ability to defeat sin and every evil in our life (1 Corinthians 10:21).

As I looked back on my journey to truth, I recognized that when I stepped out in obedience, my faith increased. When I went to a Christian conference with my sister, I stepped out in faith during the conference as they asked people to come forward that wanted to be set free or healed. I wanted to be set free; I wanted a change in my life and went forward in faith. I felt a release inside of my soul as I stepped out in faith and said no to fear. Later on in my journey, I decided to be baptized. I stepped out in obedience because I knew God wanted me to be baptized according to His word. With faith comes a corresponding action, and when we take action, it is the evidence of our faith. These acts of obedience have revealed to me how faithful God is, and how when I trust Him and walk in obedience, I am blessed.

SIN AND DISOBEDIENCE

What is sin? "So whoever knows the right thing to do and fails to do it, for him it is sin" (James 4:17). When we sin, we are harming ourselves. In Psalm 23:4, the LORD's rod and staff comfort us because they are used to protect and correct us. When there is a sheep that strays, the shepherd uses his rod and staff to keep the sheep from getting lost. The protection and correction that our Good Shepherd provides can be painful but ultimately is to keep us on the narrow path because few will find it (Proverbs 8:36, Matthew 7:14).

We are to pay attention to God's warnings. God Almighty disciplines us to save our soul from the pit. *"He brought me up also out of a horrible pit, out of the miry clay, and set my feet upon a rock, and established my goings"* (Psalm 40:2).

A man's way leads to destruction. Follow the LORD's commands, and He will be your fortress and protection. The LORD places a hedge of protection around his believers. When we sin and don't repent, this hedge of protection can break down (Job 1:10, Psalm 91).

God wants us to go to Him when we are in trouble. We think, at times, we need to use the knowledge of the world to fix our troubles. When we strive to solve our problems and exclude God, we cause more problems for ourselves. *"My son, if you will receive my words, and hide my commandments with you; So that you incline your ear to wisdom and apply your heart to understanding; Yes, if you seek after knowledge and lift up your voice for understanding; If you seek her as silver, and search for her as for hidden treasures; Then shall you understand the fear of the LORD, and find the knowledge of God. For the LORD gives wisdom: out of His mouth comes knowledge and understanding"* (Proverbs 2:1-6). I love how God says in this passage to search for His knowledge and wisdom like a hidden treasure!! I have tried to solve some of my problems without going to God first, and I end up discouraged and confused. God's ways and His solutions will bring order into our lives, and His wisdom will bring us priceless peace.

Finally, if we are continuing to sin and struggling with our own sinful desires, Psalm 119:29-40 can be used as a prayer. As we pray and turn this over to God, the Holy Spirit will lead us to confess our sin, remove the desire to sin, and cleanse us of all unrighteousness. We will also need to sow into our spiritual life (Word of God, our relationship with God, prayer, etc.) and stop sowing into our flesh (worldly desires).

When we are sowing into our flesh by worldly desires, we will reap destruction. When we sow into our spirit, we will reap life everlasting. Everything we allow into our lives, we need to evaluate if it is drawing us away from God or closer to God. All of our choices matter! *"Be not deceived, God is not mocked: for whatsoever a man sows, that shall he also reap. For he that sows to his flesh shall of the flesh reap corruption; but he that sows to the Spirit shall of the Spirit reap life everlasting"* (Galatians 6:7-8). In summary, God is the author of order. When we step outside of God's order or His protection, we are exposed and stepping outside of His covering.

PERSONAL TESTIMONY

During my truth journey, Psalm 103 has been a revelation of truth. This scripture is really a summary to me of what God has taught me about His order, His truth, and the abundant life He wants us to have. If we want to receive the abundant life God has for us, we need to be obedient to Him. Understanding the fear of the LORD is paramount. The way I describe the fear of the LORD is: knowing who God is, knowing what God says, knowing what God wants for me, and knowing what God wants of me. Therefore, from this knowledge, I choose to be obedient because He is my Heavenly Father who I love, who I know loves me and has a plan for my life.

Part of my growth process, of understanding the truth, has been recognizing the importance of the meaning of a word and how the meaning of a word can completely change what a scripture verse is saying. Psalm 103 verse 3 states, *"Who forgives all your iniquities; who heals all your diseases."* Iniquity is repetitive sin without repentance; repetitive continuing sin through family lies (generations) without repentance; and sinful thinking patterns that lead to repetitive sinning. You can examine your family tree and evaluate whether you see iniquity and determine its nature. We are to repent of iniquities. We are to recognize what iniquity is continuing through our family tree and if we are participating in it. God wants our obedience and for us to recognize the pattern of iniquity and repent (Exodus 34:7).

Psalm 103 verse 3 states, "*Who forgives **all** your iniquities; who heals **all** your diseases.*" This verse confirmed in my soul that our Heavenly Father wants us all completely healed and healthy. It is the enemy (Satan) that wants us sick.

Lastly, Psalm 103 verse 2 states, "*Bless the LORD, O my soul, and **forget not all His benefits**.*" Apparently, it was suspect that we would forget all His benefits. I don't want to forget any of them as a believer. I want all the benefits He has to offer! If I don't believe in all His benefits, how would I ever receive a benefit I didn't even have faith for?

These are the list of benefits in Psalm 103: forgives all your iniquities, heals all your diseases, redeems your life from destruction, crowns you with lovingkindness and tender mercies, satisfies your mouth with good things so that your youth is renewed like the eagle's, executes righteousness and judgment for all that are oppressed, merciful and gracious, slow to anger, abounding in mercy, and He has removed our transgression from us as far as the east is from the west.

CHAPTER 6

Our Obedience

As we follow the LORD, we will be transformed by Him. As we continue to follow and obey, we will become more holy. As God's children, we are to be set apart for the LORD. Our heart's desire will be to please God and follow Him. God will refine us, like metal is refined, to become pure. As we move from glory to glory, we will live differently from the rest of the world. There will be evidence in our lives that we are a peculiar people, set apart by God, for His purpose and plan.

God is the only one who is holy and when we abide with Him, He transforms us. As we are transformed, our desire to be like the world will be cast off, and our heart's desire will be to please God. Our appetite for our old life will be gone. There will be inward and outward evidence that we are transformed. *"A highway will be there, and a roadway; and it will be called the Holy Way. The unclean will not travel on it. But it will be for those who walk on the way [the redeemed]; and fools will not wander on it"* (Isaiah 35:8).

The world cares about our outward appearance, but the LORD cares about our inner man. The LORD looks at our hearts. What is the motive for what we are doing? Are we trying to impress others? God calls us to have a pure heart, a pure mind, a pure body, and a pure life. *"And the very God of peace sanctify you wholly; and I pray God your whole spirit and soul and body be preserved blameless to the coming of our LORD Jesus Christ"* (1 Thessalonians 5:23).

The world celebrates the outward beauty of people. The beauty industry is a 445 billion dollar industry. God looks at the inward beauty and is pleased when our heart and mind are pure. According to 1 Samuel 16:7, a man looks at the outward appearance but God looks at the heart. Proverbs 31:30 says that beauty is vain but a woman that fears the LORD, shall be praised. According to 1 Peter 3:3-4, it is of great worth to God for us to be humble in heart. God looks to see if our inner man is in order, not the appearance of our outer man.

The Pharisees opposed Jesus and His plans. Jesus rebuked the Pharisees for pride, for their religious rituals and traditions, for promoting their good works, and for advancing their personal agenda. The Pharisees cared how they appeared to the world; they didn't care how Jesus saw them. When you study the following verses in Matthew 23, you will see how it is very dangerous for us when we care about man's view of us and not God's view of us. *"Woe to you, [self-righteous] scribes and Pharisees, hypocrites! For you clean the outside of the cup and of the plate, but inside they are full of extortion and robbery and self-indulgence [unrestrained greed]. You [spiritually] blind Pharisee, first clean the inside of the cup and of the plate [examine and change your inner self to conform to God's precepts] and of the plate [examine and change your inner self to conform to God's precepts], so that the outside [your public life and deeds] may be clean also. Woe to you [self-righteous] scribes and Pharisees, hypocrites! For you are like whitewashed tombs which look beautiful on the outside, but inside are full of dead men's bones and everything unclean"* (Matthew 23:25-27). The traditions of men became the commandments the Pharisees lived by. They weren't interested in following God's commands but following what they decided was important. Their prideful attitude blinded them to God's truth. It is good to examine ourselves to determine if we are promoting our agenda or God's plans. The world loves self-promotion and pride leads the way for this behavior. When we follow God's plans, we will be moving into the highway of holiness He has planned for our life.

We as Jesus followers are to be set apart; sanctified; made holy. *"As obedient children, not conforming yourselves to the former lusts, as in your ignorance; but as He who called you is holy, you also be holy in all your conduct"* (1 Peter 1:14-15). We will not practice sinning when we follow and obey the Holy Spirit as He guides us into all truth. We are set apart for God's purpose. Our lives should appear in sharp contrast to the way unbelievers live their lives.

Through God's grace, we will have the strength and power to do God's will and move from glory to glory into the holiness He wants in our life.

Grace is the divine influence on our hearts. God's grace is His holy influence on us. His grace strengthens and empowers us to do His will.

God wants our hearts to be turned towards Him. Man thinks his ways are right, but the LORD examines the heart. In the Greek language, the word "heart" refers to a feeling, inner man, understanding, determination of will, soul. What is the condition of your heart? A cardiologist will test the condition of the heart, but God tests the condition of the heart of the inner man. *"But those things which proceed out of the mouth come forth from the heart, and they defile the man,"* (Matthew 15:18). The words that come out of our mouth will reveal the condition of our hearts. We can change our lives when we allow God to purify our hearts and then what flows out of our mouth will breathe life to ourselves and others.

"For where your treasure is, there your heart will be also," (Matthew 6:21). If our heart was a treasure box and we opened it up, what would we find? The LORD looks at our heart and cares about why we do what we do. What is our heart's motive? During Jesus's Sermon on the Mount, Jesus said that the pure in heart are blessed and that they shall see God. When you open the treasure box of your heart, do you find bitterness, hatred, lust, anger, revenge, or do you find charity, kindness, and purity? When you open the treasure box of your heart, do you find love for your enemies or are you holding hurt towards others? When the treasure box of your heart is open, do you see pride because you care about what others think? When you open the treasure box of your heart, is your heart's desire to do kingdom work for the LORD or are your thoughts on worldly rewards and pleasures? Is the treasure box of your heart revealing your fear of the future and that you are not trusting God to supply all your needs? When you look at the treasure box of your heart, do you judge others critically, or do you test yourself and evaluate if your life is pleasing to God?

God tells us to be careful that we are not causing others to stumble by our actions. Romans 14:13 says, *"Let us not therefore judge one another anymore: but judge this rather, that no man put a stumbling-block or an occasion to fall in his brother's way."* A pastor from my church stated that he and the staff abstain from alcohol so they don't cause others to stumble. These actions are a good example of protecting your Christian brother from stumbling in their faith walk. There will be things in our life that may not be a sin for us but could be a temptation for someone around us. We are set apart for God's special purpose, and we are to have a servant's heart. Making sacrifices for the LORD's purposes will be part of our faith walk. *"If a man therefore purge (cleanse) himself from these, he shall be a vessel to honor, sanctified, and meet (fit) for the master's use, and prepared to every good work"* (2 Timothy 2:21). As faithful disciples, we will come humbly before the LORD, and He will lead us on the Highway of Holiness!

PART 1 FORGIVENESS:

The Greek definition of forgiveness is a letting go, a release, pardon, complete forgiveness, releasing someone from obligation or debt. God commands us to forgive (Colossians 3:13).

Matthew 18:21-35, *"Then came Peter to him and said, 'LORD, how often shall my brother sin against me, and I forgive him? Up to seven times?' Jesus said to him, 'I do not say to you, up to seven times, but up to seventy times seven. Therefore the kingdom of heaven is like a certain king who wanted to settle accounts with his servants. And when he had begun to settle accounts, one was brought to him who owed him ten thousand talents. But as he was not able to pay, his master commanded that he be sold, with his wife and children and all that he had, and that payment be made. The servant therefore fell down before him, saying, 'Master, have patience with me, and I will pay you all.' Then the master of that servant was moved with compassion, released him, and forgave him the debt. But that servant went out and found one of his fellow servants who owed him a hundred denarii; and he laid hands on him and took him by the throat, saying, 'Pay me what you owe!' So his fellow servant fell down at his feet and begged him, saying, 'Have patience with me, and I will pay you all. And he would not, but went and threw him into prison till he should pay the debt. So when his fellow servants saw what had been done, they were very grieved, and came and told their master all that had been done. Then his master, after he had called him, said to him, 'You wicked servant! I forgave you all that debt because you begged me. Should you not also have had compassion on your fellow servant, just as I had pity on you?' And his master was angry, and delivered him to the torturers until he should pay all that was due to him. 'So My heavenly Father also will do to you if each of you, from his heart, does not forgive his brother his trespasses."* The LORD commands us to forgive others and forgive ourselves. If we don't forgive others or don't forgive ourselves, this is harmful to us. God puts no conditions on forgiving people depending on how bad the act of sin was or how many times someone sinned against us, but that we must forgive. He doesn't say we must trust them again, but we must forgive them. We need to forgive from the heart, not the head. We are to release them to God; God is the Judge.

God is the Judge and our Defender. The LORD will take care of justice; we are told by God that vengeance is not ours but God's. We are commanded to forgive and that is our part; to obediently forgive. *"Beloved, do not avenge yourselves, but rather give place to wrath; for it is written, 'Vengeance is mine, I will repay', says the LORD"* (Romans 12:19).

How do we know if we have truly forgiven someone? When we have truly forgiven someone, we will no longer have any bad feelings towards them. The sooner we forgive someone the easier this is. The longer we have had a grudge or unforgiveness it gets planted deeper in our soul and is damaging to us. If you still have bad feelings towards someone after you thought you forgave them, it is time to take a deeper look at what is going on inside of your soul and deal with it immediately. Forgiveness needs to be from the heart for it to be real forgiveness. Spend time with the LORD in prayer and repenting.

MEDICAL EVIDENCE

According to John Hopkins Medicine's Health article on Forgiveness, studies show that when we forgive people it lowers the risk of heart attack, improves cholesterol levels, improves sleep, reduces pain, improves blood pressure, helps anxiety, helps depression, and reduces stress. Dr. Karen Swartz, MD, Director of the Mood Disorders Adult Consultation Clinic, indicates how there is an "enormous physical burden to being hurt and disappointed". The article indicates that chronic anger puts us in the fight-or-flight mode which then leads to a heart rate change, blood pressure change, and immune response. Therefore, it is quite obvious from this medical information that unforgiveness and our negative emotions harm our health.

PART 2 REPENTANCE:

God leads us to repentance. Romans 2:4, *"Or do you have no regard for the wealth of His kindness and tolerance and patience [in withholding His wrath]? Are you [actually] unaware or ignorant [of the fact] that God's kindness leads you to repentance [that is, to change your inner self, your old way of thinking—seek His purpose for your life]?"*

The Greek definition of repentance is a change of mind; change in the inner man. Once we repent (change of mind), we are to confess our sins to one another so we may be healed. An example of this would be if you sinned against your spouse, the LORD wants us to confess this to our spouse. When we do this God's way, there is freedom and healing (James 5:16).

We are cleansed of all unrighteousness when we are obedient and confess our sins. According to First John 1:9-10 *"If we confess our sins, He is faithful and just to forgive us our sins and to cleanse us from all unrighteousness. If we say that we have not sinned, we make Him a liar, and His word is not in us."*

There will be times when we need to speak the truth in love to people. If the LORD leads us to speak to someone about repenting or forgiveness, 2 Timothy 2:23-26 explains how God wants us to handle this with gentle instruction.

PRAYER OF REPENTANCE: In Psalm 51 listed below, verses 1-17, this scripture can be used as a prayer of repentance. You may notice the different words used for sin which are sin, transgression, and iniquity. I have included the definitions below to clarify.

Sin = missing the mark; error.

Transgression = rebellion; a pattern of sin; knowingly sinning.

Iniquity = repetitive sin without repentance; repetitive continuing sin through family lies (generations) without repentance; sinful thinking patterns that lead to repetitive sinning.

"Have mercy upon me, O God, according to Your lovingkindness; according to the multitude of Your tender mercies, blot out my transgressions. Wash me thoroughly from my iniquity, and cleanse me from my sin. For I acknowledge my transgressions, and my sin is ever before me. Against You, You only, have I sinned, and done this evil in Your sight—that You may be justified when You speak, and clear when You Judge. Behold, I was shapen in iniquity, and in sin my mother conceived me. Behold, You desire truth in the inward parts, and in the hidden part You shall make me to know wisdom. Purge me with hyssop, and I shall be clean; wash me, and I shall be whiter than snow. Make me hear joy and gladness; that the bones You have broken may rejoice. Hide Your face from my sins, and blot out all my iniquities. Create in me a clean heart, O God; and renew a right spirit within me. Cast me not away from Your presence, and take not Your Holy Spirit from me. Restore to me the joy of Your salvation, and uphold me with Your free Spirit. Then will I teach transgressors Your ways; and sinners shall be converted to You. Deliver me from the guilt of bloodshed, O God. You God of my salvation; and my tongue shall sing aloud of Your righteousness. LORD, open you my lips; and my mouth shall show forth Your praise. For You desire not sacrifice; else I would give it; You delight not in burnt offering. The sacrifices of God are a broken spirit; a broken and a contrite heart—O God, You will not despise" (Psalm 51:1-17).

CHAPTER 7

True Identity or Stolen Identity

Just like your personal information can be stolen by a credit card thief, a hacker, or scammer; your identity can be stolen. Satan comes to steal, and he will go to great lengths to take what is yours, including who God created you to be. Do you know your true identity or has your identity been stolen by sin, by Satan, or by the world? When you know your Creator, you will know how beautifully He made you and who He says you are!! Don't let the world define your identity. You can't trust the world or others to define your identity. Don't let Satan deceive you and get you to believe lies about yourself. We are made in God's image. We are all unique and created to be ourselves, and no one else is like us. God wants us to know who we are in Jesus Christ. The only one who knows the purpose and plans for your life is our Creator. He formed you in your mother's womb and made plans for your life. *"Before I formed you in the womb I knew you; before you were born I sanctified you; . . ."* (Jeremiah 1:5). If we allow sin, Satan, or the world to deceive us and steal our true identity, we won't know the potential and possibilities that our Heavenly Father had waiting for us.

Don't agree with who the world says you need to be. Don't agree with the lies in your head that you are not good enough. Don't agree with the negative words others say about you. What you agree with is really important because an agreement with lies will lead to a stolen identity, while an agreement with the truth about who God made you to be will lead you to your true identity.

How are you identified by your Heavenly Father? Our Heavenly Father knows us better than our mother or father, better than our husband or wife, better than our brother or sister, better than our children, and better than our life long best friend. The LORD knows our thoughts, our hearts, and even the number of hairs on our heads. He created each of us and knows the plans He has for us. Jesus said in Matthew 10:39 that whoever loses his life for His sake, will find it. When we live for the LORD, we will know who we are. We will know our identity when we know Jesus Christ.

God knows when we sit down and when we rise up. He knows our thoughts. He knows the words we speak. He formed us in our mother's womb. He planned out our days before we were born. But if we never follow God's will for our life, we never find the days He had planned for us and how wonderful they would have been. Since God made our inner being, He knows what we are created for and what makes our soul and spirit flourish. If we follow His lead, we will have the peace He intended us to have. Don't let the world steal your identity and rob you of your destiny. There is a special, very specific, plan God has for your life. If we follow the world, we will be seduced into self-indulgence, comfort, security, etc., and we miss the destiny God has planned for us.

How does Jesus know His children? Jesus said, *"My sheep hear My voice, and I know them, and they follow Me."* We are His children when He knows us, and when we know Him and follow Him. Then we have our eternal identity in Him and will be with Him forever. The world will only know us by what we choose to expose and the image we have created. But our Heavenly Father knows everything about us. There is nothing that we need to hide from God. He knows everything about us so why not go to Him and trust Him. That is where you will find your identity when you confide in your Heavenly Father and trust Him. He has unconditional love for us. God wants us to talk to Him, and He will help us with everything in our lives if we only let Him in. He wants to direct us and lead us into a better life of obedience to Him. No one on this earth will ever love us the way our Heavenly Father does.

The world is our taskmaster. If we are listening to the world and following the world, when we arrive at our destination of fame and glory, we find it was all a mirage. The worldly pleasures appeal to our immediate gratification, but when we arrive, we feel empty inside; unfulfilled. We were made for so much more. True fulfillment is when we follow the LORD and His plans for our life. When you look at King Solomon's life from the Bible, he had incredible wisdom, he was King of Israel, he had 700 wives, he was wealthy with palaces and gold, but when Solomon reached old age he wrote how his life was meaningless. King Solomon concluded in Ecclesiastes 12:13-14, *"Let us hear the conclusion of the whole matter: Fear God, and keep His commandments: for this is the whole duty of man. For God shall bring every work into judgment, with every secret thing, whether it be good, or whether it be evil."* The LORD had warned King Solomon that if he married women that followed other gods that it would lead him astray. Solomon's heart led him to follow his lust for wealth and women. He found out at the end of his life how it was all meaningless. Solomon had lost his true identity in the LORD. He followed his worldly pleasures into a meaningless life.

How do we protect our identity? We protect our identity by keeping our eyes on our Heavenly Father and seeking His will for our life. God looks at our hearts. The world will seduce you into believing the outward appearance is vitally important, but God wants a humble heart. When your heart is pure, you will follow the LORD and know your identity. You will then follow God into the abundant life He has for you. This better life will be meaningful and lead to everlasting peace. Your true identity will bring you peace and joy!

CHAPTER 8

Bringing Heaven to Earth (Prayer)

When we pray, we are bringing heaven to earth. *"Thy kingdom come. Thy will be done in earth, as it is in heaven,"* according to Matthew 6:10. As sons and daughters of the King, we establish God's kingdom here on earth. God gives His authority to His believers to bring His kingdom to the earth. When we pray, we are appropriating Jesus Christ's completed work on the cross to our own lives and to those we pray for.

The Word of God is living and powerful, and is the main way God communicates with us. Reading, studying, and meditating on the Word of God helps us hear God more clearly. It is like when you are waiting to hear from someone you love and you keep your phone close by and turn the volume up so you don't miss the call. The Word of God is alive and active waiting to speak to us. When we are talking to God in prayer, don't shut your phone off after you are done talking to God. Allow God time to speak back to you and give you direction.

If you are unclear on how to pray, the Word of God is your guide. When we know the Word of God, we will know God's will for our lives and how to pray. God knows what is best for His children and wants us to trust Him. We are told in the Word of God to cast our cares on Him. Therefore, we are not to worry but release our concerns to Him and pray.

In the spirit realm, the answer to our prayer is yes and amen if we are praying God's will. Our faith works in the spiritual realm to bring our prayers to pass. Faith and prayer go hand in hand. Our enemy, Satan, wants us to be discouraged and doubt; and therefore, not pray or pray in unbelief and doubt. Our prayers in faith move the power of heaven. According to Daniel 10, Daniel's prayer was answered in heaven but was held up getting to him because of the evil kingdom battling against him. When we pray, we get resistance from the kingdom of darkness because of the conflict between good and evil. Satan wants us to give up and lose heart, but stand in faith praying (battling) to bring heaven to earth. This is our assignment (Mark 11:24).

BELOW ARE SOME TYPES OF PRAYERS FROM THE WORD OF GOD:

(1) <u>Faith prayer</u>. Mark 11:24 states, *"Therefore I say unto you, what things soever you desire, when you pray, believe that you receive them, and you shall have them."* The prayer in faith may seem obvious but you should look at your heart and examine if there is doubt or unbelief when you pray. When you spend time with God in His word and listen to the testimonies of God's faithfulness in your life and others, this will help remove any doubt or unbelief. Your prayer of faith should be spoken out loud because *"faith comes by hearing"* (Romans 10:17).

(2) <u>Prayer of Agreement</u>. Matthew 18:19 says, *"Again I say unto you, that if two of you shall agree on earth as touching anything that they shall ask, it shall be done for them of my Father which is in heaven."* Since this is the prayer of agreement, make sure both prayer partners are in complete agreement on the prayer request.

(3) <u>Binding and loosing prayer</u>. According to Matthew 18:18, *"Verily I say unto you, whatever you shall bind on earth shall be bound in heaven: and whatsoever you shall loose on earth shall be loosed in heaven."* Use your spiritual authority to loose the bands of wickedness by prayer and fasting according to Isaiah 58. In Luke 13:12, Jesus loosed a woman of her infirmity. An example of a binding prayer; "I bind the strongman causing strife in my family, no weapon formed against my family will prosper."

(4) <u>Intercessory prayer</u>. A prayer of intercession is when we are praying to God for other's needs. If you ask others to pray for you, you are giving your authority (your free will) for others to cover you in prayer (James 5:16, 1 Timothy 2:1).

(5) <u>Praising and thanking God in prayer</u>. Thanking and praising God removes the lies of unbelief and doubt and fills our hearts with His goodness (Philippians 4:6, Ephesians 5:19-20).

(6) <u>Praying in tongues</u>. Praying in tongues is a gift from God and can be a wonderful way to pray for something or someone when you are not sure how to pray (1 Corinthians 14:2, Acts 2:4).

(7) <u>The LORD's Prayer</u> (Matthew 6:9-15).

(8) <u>Prayers from the heart</u> (Proverbs 3:5, Psalm 51:10).

(9) <u>Spiritual Warfare Prayer</u>. See the Chapter on *Our Spiritual Warfare* for details on this type of prayer.

GOD'S ORDER IN PRAYER

God is a God of order and understanding His order will help you in your prayer life:

1) After Jesus rose from the dead, we are to pray to God the Father, and we are to pray in the name of Jesus (John 14:12-13). *"And in that day you will ask Me nothing. Most assuredly, I say to you, whatever you ask the Father in My name He will give you"* (John 16:23).

2) We as believers have been given spiritual authority in Jesus's name to conduct His business here on earth. We are to bring heaven to earth. According to John 14:12-14, *"Verily, verily, I say unto you, He that believeth on me, the works that I do shall he do also; and greater works than these shall he do; because I go unto my Father. And whatsoever ye shall ask in my name, that will I do, that the Father may be glorified in the Son. If ye shall ask anything in my name, I will do it."*

3) Our prayers can be hindered by our wrong motives (James 4:3), our sin (Proverbs 28:9, Isaiah 59:2, John 9:31), our unforgiveness (Mark 11:25), our unconfessed sin (Psalm 66:18), our unbelief (James 1:5-7), or a husband's discord with his wife (1 Peter 3:7).

4) We are to be persistent in our requests to God. The LORD's word says, *"because of his persistence He will rise and give him as many as he needs"* (Luke 11:8-13).

5) We need to pray in faith. When we pray in unbelief, we will not see our prayers answered. According to Mark 11:24, *"whatever things you ask when you pray, believe that you receive them, and you will have them."*

6) When we ask God for something in prayer, we should always thank God after we pray (Philippians 4:6).

7) Daily prayer is essential. Also, we should pray daily in the Spirit (speaking in tongues) since the Spirit knows what to pray (1 Thessalonians 5:16-18, Ephesians 6:18).

A.) THE WORD OF GOD IS SHARPER THAN ANY TWO-EDGED SWORD.

"For the Word of God is quick, and powerful, and sharper than any two-edged sword, piercing even to the dividing asunder of soul and spirit, and of the joints and marrow, and is a discerner of the thoughts and intents of the heart" (Hebrews 4:12). Below are some specific prayers and examples of decrees using the Word of God. A decree is an official order issued by a legal authority. Job 22:28 says we shall decree a thing, and it will be established to us. When we make a decree, we believe what we are saying in our hearts, and we know the authority we have as believers in Jesus, the LORD says our decree will be established to us!!

1) Decree: You are fearfully and wonderfully made. If something is trying to come against your health or future, decree what God's word says about His marvelous works in your life.

"For You formed my inward parts; You covered me in my mother's womb. I will praise You, for I am fearfully and wonderfully made; Marvelous are Your works, and that my soul knows very well. My frame was not hidden from You, when I was made in secret, And skillfully wrought in the lowest parts of the earth. Your eyes saw my substance, being yet unformed. And in Your book they all were written, The days fashioned for me, When as yet there were none of them" (Psalm 139:13-16).

2) Decree: We serve the LORD. If Satan is trying to gain a foothold in a family member's life, decree this verse and put Satan on notice that your family serves the LORD. *". . . As for me and my house, we will serve the LORD"* (Joshua 24:15).

3) Spiritual warfare prayers using the Word of God:

"And the LORD will deliver me from every evil work and preserve me for His heavenly kingdom. To Him be glory forever and ever. Amen!" (2 Timothy 4:18)

"For You have delivered my soul from death, my eyes from tears, and my feet from falling" (Psalm 116:8).

"The LORD will cause your enemies who rise against you to be defeated before your face; they shall come out against you one way and flee before you seven ways " (Deuteronomy 28:7).

In the Name of Jesus Christ by the power of His blood, I break off every power of darkness and cancel every argument that has established itself against the plans of God in the lives of my family and my life (2 Corinthians 10:5-7).

"No weapon that is formed against you shall prosper; and every tongue that shall rise against you in judgment you shall condemn. This is the heritage of the servants of the LORD, and their righteousness is of Me, says the LORD" (Isaiah 54:17).

4) Prayer when tempted. Pray that the LORD will provide a way of escape when you are tempted. *"There has no temptation taken you but such as is common to man: but God is faithful, who will not suffer (permit) you to be tempted above that you are* able; but will with the temptation also make a way to escape, that you may be able to bear it" (1 Corinthians 10:13).

5) Prayer for a peaceful sleep.
Psalm 4:8, *"I will both lay me down in peace, and sleep: for you, LORD, only make me dwell in safety."*
Proverbs 3:24-26, *"When you lie down, you shall not be afraid: yea, you shall lie down, and your sleep shall be sweet. Be not afraid of sudden fear, neither of the desolation of the wicked, when it comes. For the LORD shall be your confidence, and shall keep your foot from being taken."*

6) Prayer for knowledge from the LORD. If you are seeking the LORD for a piece of knowledge you need (For example a word of wisdom or knowledge for a situation) you can use Jeremiah 33:3, *"Call on Me, and I will answer you, and show you great and mighty things, which you do not know."*

7) Prayers, for the salvation of an unbeliever, using the Word of God:
2 Timothy 2:26: *"and that they may recover themselves out of the snare of the devil, who are taken captive by him at his will."*
Hebrews 4:16: *"Let us therefore come boldly to the throne of grace, that we may obtain mercy, and find grace to help in time of need."*
Dear LORD your word says according to John 6:44, *"No one can come to Me, except the Father which has sent Me draw him: and I will raise him up at the last day."*
"Pray you therefore the LORD of the harvest, that He will send forth laborers into His harvest" (Matthew 9:38).

8) Prayer for God to direct your steps. God has a plan for our life. Satan has a plan for our life also. We need to pray and ask God for His guidance, for the right timing and direction, so we don't move out of God's destiny for our lives. We make plans but He directs our steps. *"Trust in the LORD with all thine heart; and lean not unto thine own understanding. In all thy ways acknowledge Him, and He shall direct thy paths"* (Proverbs 3:5-6).

9) Pray over your food.
1 Timothy 4:1-5, *"Now the Spirit speaketh expressly, that in the latter times some shall depart from the faith, giving heed to seducing spirits, and doctrines of devils; Speaking lies in hypocrisy; having their conscience seared with a hot iron; Forbidding to marry, and commanding to abstain from meats, which God hath created to be received with thanksgiving of them which believe and know the truth. For every creature of God is good, and nothing to be refused, if it be received with thanksgiving: For it is sanctified by the Word of God and prayer."* Don't allow Satan to gain any ground on the food you eat

or your drink. The Word of God says to pray before we eat or drink and our food is blessed to our bodies.

There are verses in the Bible regarding food that I don't understand their full truth yet. But various places in the Bible indicate there is food that has been offered to idols, and we may not even be aware of this. Therefore, we need to pray over everything we eat that it is blessed (1 Corinthians 8:4-9). Another scripture verse speaks about how some people believe in their heart they can eat anything, while others only vegetables (Romans 14:1-4). In summary, we need to pray over our food according to 1 Corinthians 10:31 and Acts 27:35.

B) FASTING AND PRAYER

When we decide to fast, we are choosing to abstain from food for some time usually for a specific reason either to seek wisdom, worship, repent, protection, healing, deliverance, etc. In our Christian walk, there will be sacrifices we will make when we are obedient to our Heavenly Father. Whenever we give up our free will to be obedient to Him, we are trusting in the LORD and acknowledging Him in our ways, and He will make our path straight (Proverbs 3:5-6).

According to the Word of God, the disciples of Jesus Christ are to fast and pray (Luke 5:33-35). We fast and pray to:

1) Seek the wisdom of God according to Acts 14:23.
2) Prepare for ministry according to Mark 1:12-13 and Luke 4:1-14.
3) Seek counsel, protection, or deliverance according to Ezra 8:21-23 and Judges 20:23-28.
4) Repent according to Jonah 3.
5) Worship according to Luke 2:37-38.
6) Achieve victory according to 2 Chronicles 20:1-25.

Our Heavenly Father knows our heart, and if we are fasting with the wrong heart motive, He is not pleased (Isaiah 58). He wants us to come humbly before Him and sorrowfully repent of any unrighteousness. Our Heavenly Father does not want us to fast as a religious ritual. When we come to God with the right heart, we respond in love and obedience, and this is what God wants. *"Therefore also now, says the LORD, turn you even to Me with all your heart, and with fasting, and with weeping, and with mourning: And rend (tear) your heart, and not your garments, and turn to the LORD your God"* (Joel 2:12-13a).

When we are fasting, we are more easily able to hear and be led by the Holy Spirit while we are setting our needs of the flesh aside. *"One day as these men were worshipping the LORD and fasting, the Holy Spirit said, 'Appoint Barnabus and Saul for the special work to which I have called them'"* (Acts 13:2).

As believers, we are to have self-control. 2 Timothy 1:7 says, *"For God gave us a spirit not of fear but of power and love and self-control."* When we fast, we have an opportunity to exercise our self-control. Exercising our self-control will increase our ability to have self-control. During a recent fast, God was teaching me restraint and to pay attention to my impulse to eat. I was recognizing that when I started to imagine a certain kind of food and how wonderful it would taste, I had a strong desire to eat it. Therefore, I became very aware of my thoughts during this fast. I needed to cast down imaginations and every high thing that exalts itself against the knowledge of God according to 2 Corinthians 10:5. This particular fast showed me the power of the imagination, and I needed to be intentional in using my imagination for God's good purposes.

In Matthew 17:14-21, the disciples were not able to cure a boy that was greatly oppressed. Jesus indicates in verse 21 *"however this kind goes not out but by prayer and fasting"*. If there are situations in your life that you have not been able to overcome, they may require fasting and prayer because of the level of spiritual evil. According to Ephesians 6:12, there are different levels of the spiritual kingdom.

Isaiah 58 is an amazing scripture teaching on fasting. You will want to read this for yourself, but I will highlight some points. When we are fasting, the LORD wants us to be discrete, humble, and stop sinning. The LORD wants us to serve and give to those in need while we are fasting. When we fast the LORD's way, the fast will *"loose the bands of wickedness, do the heavy burdens, and to let the oppressed go free, and that you break every yoke?"*

Minister Kevin L. A. Ewing has a teaching called <u>Understanding the Mystery of Fasting</u> on YouTube. This is a wonderful teaching on fasting and contains many scripture verses to explain some of the mysteries of fasting that you may not have been taught.

PERSONAL TESTIMONY-THE POWER OF PRAYER

About twenty years ago, I prayed to the LORD that I would have a closer relationship with my brother. Since my brother was 13 years younger, there was an obvious age difference while we were growing up. Secondly, while he was in high school, I lived in another state and wasn't able to go to his high school baseball and football games. My heart's desire was to be able to attend those events and be a part of those important parts of his life, but this didn't happen. This led me to my prayer request years later when I asked God to build a close relationship between me and my brother. I lived in Michigan, at the time, and my brother lived in Arizona. About a year and a half later, my husband received a job transfer to Arizona. I had never even considered moving to Arizona. God moved our family to Arizona and my husband's job was across the street from my brother's job. Also, my brother's house and our house in Arizona were within 5 miles of each other. These towns had populations around 150,000 at that time and for God to place us that close together was amazing. What an awesome God! One of the loveliest things about living in Arizona was that my brother was there, He was a significant part of our family's life in Arizona, and my children loved having their Uncle Mark spend time with them. This will always be a treasured time for me. God answers our prayers in the most perfect and unexpected ways!

ANOTHER PERSONAL TESTIMONY- THE POWER OF PRAYER

When we were in the process of selling our Arizona home of 17 years, it was on my heart that a family with children would buy our home. We had raised our children there and had such wonderful memories, and I wanted another family to be blessed by our home. I had prayed that the LORD would provide the right family to purchase our home. After about a month and a half on the market, an investor made an offer to buy our home. He was going to do some renovating and probably use it as an investment property. This was not what I wanted or what I prayed for, but we decided to sell to him since no other offers came, and we needed to relocate for my husband's job. About four days before closing day, our real estate agent called us, and the loan for this man fell through. Our home went back on the market. Our movers came, and we moved out of our home in Arizona. About a month and a half later, we had another offer on our home. It was a family with young children who owned a local restaurant. The community supported this family and their local business as they hired young adults with autism for their workforce. When our agent called to tell me this, I was overjoyed that God answered my prayer in such a beautiful way. Sometimes our prayers may take a little more time to answer because God is working out the details we don't see. My heart was full as I was in my new home and reflecting on the answered prayer by God. It brought me peace that God had a beautiful family lined up to move into our home. God cares about the little and big matters of our heart!

CHAPTER 9

Our Superpower: The Power of Faith

First of all, who is your faith in, and what are you believing for? My faith is in Jesus Christ and the completed work He has done on the cross. I believe in the Word of God. If someone does not know the Word of God and have it planted in their heart, how can they activate it by faith? And Jesus said to His disciples. *"Go you into all the world and preach the gospel to every creature. He that believes and is baptized shall be saved: but he that believes not shall be damned. And these signs shall follow them that believe: In My name shall they cast out devils; they shall speak with new tongues; They shall take up serpents; and if they drink any deadly thing, it shall not hurt them; they shall lay hands on the sick, and they shall recover"* (Mark 16:15-18).

Faith is the substance of things hoped for and the evidence of things not seen. Faith activates the Word of God and brings heaven to earth. When we stand in faith, we will see the glory of God! If we stay wise in the eyes of the world, we stay in darkness. We need to be willing to be foolish in the eyes of the world because the world lives by what they see in the physical. For those who live by faith, there will be evidence of their faith in their actions and words (Hebrew 11:1, John 11:40).

All believers have been given "a measure of faith". Faith is a gift from God, and we are to exercise this gift. What evidence is there of your faith? *". . . who makes alive the dead, and calls those things which be not as though they were",*

Romans 4:17. If faith has no proof, is it faith? What evidence is there of your faith? If you were in a court of law, what evidence would you bring forward to prove your faith?

Faith questions to ask ourselves:
1) Who do I trust for my daily provision?
2) Do the choices I make reveal I have faith in God?
3) Am I embarrassed or timid in what I believe?
4) What evidence is there in my life that I trust God with my life?

Faith is the confidence we have in what we hope for, and faith is the proof of things not seen. In Hebrews 11, the Word of God speaks about the men and women of faith and how when they died, they were in the faith. We are to live a life of faith. Verse 3 explains that through faith the world was created by the Word of God from things not seen by God. Noah prepared the ark being warned by God of things not seen yet. There will be proof in our lives of our faith, by the confidence we have, in what we hope for. It is impossible to please God without faith.

FAITH VERSUS FEAR

If you choose to live by fear, you will have torment. First John 4:18 states, *"There is no fear in love; but perfect love casteth out fear because fear hath torment. He hath feareth is not made perfect in love."* When you are spending time with God and experiencing His perfect love, fear will be driven out.

Fear and faith operate in the spiritual realm. Faith brings the Kingdom of Light and fear (spirit of fear from Satan) brings the kingdom of darkness. If you believe what God's word says about you and are standing on His promises, you are agreeing with God and standing in faith for this for your future. If you are living in fear, you are agreeing with what Satan wants in your life which is to steal, kill, and destroy the plans God has for you. Stop projecting fear for your future and project faith! (Job 3:25) When God showed me that being fearful was agreeing with the enemy (Satan), I was in amazement of the deception that I did not recognize! I was agreeing with darkness, not the light.

When we have faith in the things of God, we will speak faith. The same is true when you walk in fear. Fear will be shown by what you speak. Your words will either show evidence of fear or faith. Test your words and determine what the evidence proves (Mark 11:22-24, Proverbs 18:21).

If you are in a state of fear regularly, you are showing that you don't trust God. If you do not trust God, you are sinning. It is not possible to please God if you are without faith. Faith stands for your future. Fear can destroy your future. Faith comes by hearing; therefore, read the Word of God out loud to build your faith (Romans 8:15).

When we have fear, stress, or anxiety, it can cause havoc in our body, mind and soul. This is a high price to pay when you remain in fear. We need to stand in faith, not fear. We should periodically evaluate our thoughts and actions to determine if they are aligning with the Word of God. If we find we are allowing fear and anxiety to direct our life, we need to make a course adjustment. We can start with recognizing the wrong direction we are going, repent to God for agreeing with fear, and renounce fear. We can make a declaration of peace over our lives, and pray that the LORD directs our steps in the direction He wants us to go. We should be purposefully listening to God for direction and what course adjustments we need to make. When we surrender to God and wait on Him for the answer, He will direct us (Matthew 6:25-34, Philippians 4:6-7).

We are not to fear evil. We are not to fear man. We are not to fear the terror of the night. We are not to fear other gods. We are to have faith and be strong and courageous! Evaluate and test yourself as to whether you are responding in courage and letting God lead your life, or are you agreeing with Satan and letting fear direct your steps (Psalm 91:5-6, Deuteronomy 31:6).

If you have meditated long enough on fear, you have made a pathway for fear. You need to recognize how fear has gained access in your mind and rebuke it. Renew your mind with the Word of God. How do I rebuke fear and renew my mind? 1) Recognize that fear is a liar. Recognize how fear got access to you so you can say no when it shows up again. 2) Speak to your fear, "Fear I rebuke and renounce you, you have no place here, get out fear!" 3) Repent to the LORD for agreeing with fear. 4) Make a list of the fears in your mind. 5) Search the scriptures for the truth that rebukes the fear. 6) Speak the truths you found in the scriptures and continue to meditate on them until they become planted in your mind and heart (Ephesians 4:23, Romans 12:2).

If we want the LORD's plans for our lives to be fulfilled, we need to walk by faith. If we walk in fear, Satan's plans for our lives may be fulfilled. For as you think in your heart, you are. What do you believe in your heart about yourself and your life? Do you believe what God says about you or are you agreeing with the lies of the enemy? Write out the plans for your life. Test your plans and make sure they don't disagree with the Word of God. Then put your plans before the LORD, and ask Him to direct your steps. (1 Peter 5:8, Proverbs 3:5-6).

Our Shield of Faith stops the attacks from Satan. The more you abide in the LORD and the things of His kingdom, your faith will abound. Believers can stand together and fight the faith battle together. We are to courageously fight the good fight of faith (Ephesians 6:16).

PERSONAL TESTIMONY

Fear had me captive for many, many years. I wasn't even aware that fear imprisoned me until I was free. I had a bad case of fear of man; I cared way too much what people thought about me. I was afraid of failure. I made poor decisions because I was basing some decisions on what man thought and not what God thought. God has set me free from this darkness. When I look back, I didn't love myself, and I didn't even know that I was supposed to love myself. Satan is a liar and his deception and lies have been exposed. I am a child of God and my identity is in Him. I want to please God, not man. I renounce fear and fear you have no power over me! God has a plan for my life, and I can't waste any more time on the lies of Satan. I choose to listen to God and walk out His plan for my life.

PRAYING IN FAITH

Faith is how we receive any promise the LORD has placed in His Word. *"That you be not slothful, but followers of them who through faith and patience inherit the promises"* (Hebrews 6:12). We receive salvation by faith. All things through Christ are done by faith. We are overcomers by faith as we stand on the promises of God. *"For whatsoever is born of God overcomes the world: and this is the victory that overcomes the world, even our faith"* (1 John 5:4).

Your faith can completely change your situation and other people's lives. Matthew 8:13 *"Go! It will be done just as you believed it would."* Take a moment to deeply reflect on the power of faith and how lives can be changed when we believe! There is an amazing YouTube video of Margy Mayfield and how her faith gave her the strength to witness to a serial killer who had abducted her and how he gave his life to Christ that day. I would encourage you to watch this video.

"Now faith is the substance of things hoped for, the evidence of things not seen. . ." (Hebrews 11:1-3). Your actions that are done in faith and the words you speak in faith will be evidence of your faith. Your words and actions in doubt will be evidence of your unbelief.

When you speak in faith, you are not trying to convince yourself or someone else of something. In the spiritual realm, faith is the fuel that moves things in the supernatural. You are putting your faith to work! You are calling things that are not, as though they were. Faith is your free will operating and saying "yes God, I believe what you have promised, I believe your Word in my heart" (Ephesians 6:16, Romans 4:17).

Our faith is what moves things from the spiritual realm (heaven) to the physical realm (earth). If our prayer request is so big that we can't even imagine it ever happening, this will be a big stumbling block for our faith. When I am struggling to imagine the answer to my prayer, I listen to the testimonies of faith and read scriptures revealing God's power. God created us with imaginations and using our imaginations the way God intended is powerful. Use your imagination to see your victory as an overcomer. Meditate, imagine, and visualize your victory as an overcomer (Matthew 9:29, Colossians 3:2).

When you are standing in faith for the answer to your prayer, remove fear and doubt from your thoughts. You can't control the thoughts that come into your mind, but you can cast the wrong thoughts out of your mind. Be intentional about what you allow yourself to meditate on. Meditate on God's word and His promises to you. Feed (sow) your spiritual life, and do not feed (sow) your flesh with worldly things because you will reap what you sow into (Joshua 1:8, Galatians 5:16-24).

We are told in 1 Corinthians 16:13 to stand fast in the faith. *"Watch you, stand fast in the faith, quit you (act) like men, be strong."* This verse indicates we are to watch and stand fast. These are actions of persisting, persevering, strict attention, being watchful, and standing strong as a believer. This is similar to a soldier standing on watch at his post; the soldier can't fall asleep because he has a job to do. The disciple of Jesus Christ puts his faith to work. Our faith has an assignment.

Keep speaking each day what you want according to God's will, not what you see in front of you. Anyone can speak what is here in the earthly realm, but a person of faith speaks what they want to come to pass according to God's will. We are prophesying our future by what we speak in faith. As you think in your heart, so you are. Seek the LORD and what He says about you and believe it (Proverbs 23:7, Micah 7:7).

When we are speaking in faith, we are not denying the facts that exist in a situation. We are to always speak the truth. But as believers, we know with God all things are possible, and despite what facts exist in the physical realm, we know what is possible with God. We need to agree with God's plans for our life and renounce Satan's plans.

We are to continue to stand in faith, regardless of how long we are standing in faith. Our faith has an assignment and faith does not have an expiration date. In Hebrews 11*:13, "These all died in faith, not having received the promises, but having seen them afar off, and were persuaded of them, and embraced them, and confessed that they were strangers and pilgrims on the earth."*

CHAPTER 10

Our Guide

After we have received Jesus Christ as our LORD and Savior, the Holy Spirit dwells in us. The Holy Spirit speaks to our spirit. We are spirit beings with a body, mind, and soul. Our body is the house that holds our spirit, soul, and mind.

At salvation, we are born again and new creations. *"If you declare with your mouth, 'Jesus is LORD' and believe in your heart that God raised Him from the dead, you will be saved. For it is with your heart that you believe and are justified, and it is with your mouth that you profess your faith and are saved"* (Romans 10:9-10). When you believe in your heart Jesus is your LORD and Savior and confess with your mouth, you are saved. To believe Jesus is to trust Him, follow Him, and obey Him. *"Therefore, if anyone is in Christ, he is a new creation; old things have passed away; behold, all things have become new"* (2 Corinthians 5:17). The Holy Spirit transforms us as He counsels and guides us on our walk of faith.

Once a person believes and confesses that Jesus Christ is their LORD and Savior, the believer is to be water baptized as an outward act of obedience after salvation. Water baptism is an outward expression of an inner change; the old man is dead and the new man arises. We become a new creation. The baptism of the Holy Spirit is a separate spiritual experience from water baptism.

After Jesus received the baptism of the Holy Spirit, He manifested the power of God by preaching, healing, and casting out demons. Keeping in mind that Jesus, the Son of God, came to earth as a man; Jesus's life went from natural to supernatural after He was baptized in the Holy Spirit. In Acts 8:14-17, it explains that water baptism and the baptism of the Holy Spirit are two separate experiences. How do I receive the baptism of the Holy Spirit? Luke 11:10-13 explains that we ask the Father for the Holy Spirit, and we will receive. In Act 8:14-17, you will see Peter and John prayed for those that asked to receive the Holy Spirit, and then they placed their hands on them, and they received the Holy Spirit. When we ask the LORD for the baptism of the Holy Spirit, we will receive the power to do His kingdom work which His disciples are commissioned to do (Acts 2:1-4, Matthew 3:11 "... *He shall baptize you with the Holy Ghost and with fire*").

Once Jesus received the baptism of the Holy Spirit (power of the Holy Spirit), He began His ministry of preaching, healing, and casting out demons (Matthew 3:16-17). Jesus, the Son of God, received the power of the Holy Spirit (Baptism of the Holy Spirit) before starting His ministry. Likewise, His followers need the power of the Holy Spirit to be effective disciples for the LORD (Acts 2:1-4). In Acts 1:4-5 and Acts 1:8-9, the disciples were told by Jesus to wait until they were baptized in the Holy Spirit before they began their ministry. We should follow this example and be baptized in the Holy Spirit.

I was baptized as an infant by the sprinkling of water on my forehead. Much later in life at the age of 45, I had learned the importance of water baptism by immersion and was baptized. Continuing in my truth journey, the LORD taught me about the baptism of the Holy Spirit. I came to understand and believe, according to God's word, that the baptism of the Holy Spirit was something I could ask the LORD for and receive. I went to a healing room, and they laid hands on me and anointed me with oil. They asked me if I spoke in tongues, and if not, if I wanted to be baptized in the Holy Spirit. I told them I wanted to be baptized in the Holy Spirit. They prayed over me to receive the baptism of the Holy Spirit. I began to speak in tongues which is an outward sign after receiving the baptism of the Holy Spirit, according to the book of Acts.

According to Luke 11:13, the baptism of the Holy Spirit is a gift, not something that you earn. *"If you then being evil, know how to give good gifts to your children: how much more shall your heavenly Father give the Holy Spirit to them that ask Him?"* (Luke 11:13). The Holy Spirit empowers us with truth and power to do His work of preaching, casting out demons, speaking in new tongues, and healing the sick. According to Acts 2:1-4, one of the first manifestations of being baptized in the Holy Spirit was speaking in tongues.

Speaking in tongues was evidence in the Book of Acts that the disciples were baptized in the Holy Spirit (Acts 10:44-46, Acts 11:15-18, Acts 19:6). When someone speaks in tongues, it is their spirit speaking. The Holy Spirit gives our spirit the words to speak. Speaking in tongues releases power into our life for spiritual growth. You speak the hidden wisdom of God when you speak in tongues. *"For he that speaks in an unknown tongue speaks not to men, but to God: for no man understands him; however in the spirit he speaks mysteries"* (1 Corinthians 14:2). When you speak in tongues, you edify yourself. First Corinthians 14:4 says, *"He that speaketh in an unknown tongue edifies himself. . ."* In Greek, the word 'edifies' means to build up from the foundation; to promote growth in Christian wisdom, grace, affection, holiness, and blessedness.

In Acts 2:1-11, the disciples were baptized in the Holy Spirit on Pentecost. "The disciples were *filled with the Holy Ghost, and began to speak with other tongues, as the Spirit gave them utterance*" (Acts 2:4). First Corinthians 14:2 states, *"For he that speaks in an unknown tongue speaks not to men, but to God: for no man understands him; however in the spirit he speaks mysteries."* First Corinthians 13:1 states, *"Though I speak with the tongues of men and angels. . ."* First Corinthians 12:10 explains tongues as various kinds of tongues. As I am studying these verses, to the best of my understanding, the tongues of men are the gift of speaking in tongues that enables you to speak an earthly language that you never learned. Speaking tongues of angels, in my understanding, is the speaking of tongues that is a heavenly language available to all Spirit-baptized believers. I have friends that speak an earthly language (the tongues of men) that they never learned, and they received after being baptized in the Holy Spirit.

The Holy Spirit guides us into all truth. God's truth and His revelation became clearer to me after baptism (immersion) and even more understanding of His truth after being baptized in the Holy Spirit. As I matured spiritually, wrong thinking patterns were removed and the truth flourished. As I studied God's word, I had a deeper understanding of God's truth than before, and I could discern things clearer. *"However, when He, the Spirit of Truth, has come, He will guide you into all truth, for He will not speak on His own authority, but whatever He hears He will speak, and He will tell you things to come. He will glorify Me, for He will take of what is Mine and declare it to you"* (John 16:13-14).

The Holy Spirit empowers us with His power to live an overcomer's life and to help others to overcome. The Holy Spirit empowers us with gifts. In 1 Corinthians 12:8-11, these verses list the gifts of the Holy Spirit which are: word of wisdom, word of knowledge, faith, gifts of healing, working of miracles, prophecy, discerning of spirits, various kinds of tongues, and the interpretation of tongues. These gifts of the Holy Spirit display God's glory and power here on earth to help us overcome.

We have spiritual discernment by the power of the Holy Spirit and the Word of God. Discernment is the ability to recognize good from evil. We must be able to discern between God's truth and Satan's lies. We need to know the Word of God for ourselves and test all teachings or thoughts against the Word of God. The Holy Spirit is the Spirit of Truth and will lead us to the truth. We are to receive the truth and follow it with obedient actions (John 14:17, 2 Corinthians 10:5).

Satan is the deceiver and counterfeiter. Satan's kingdom has levels of evil: principalities, powers, rulers of the darkness of this world, and spiritual wickedness in high places. Part of the deception of the evil kingdom is displaying counterfeit powers. As you read in Exodus 7, Moses and Aaron cast their rod before Pharaoh, and it became a serpent. Then Pharaoh brought forward his sorcerers (magicians), and they also cast their rod, and it became a serpent. But then Aaron's rod swallowed up their rods. Satan and his evil kingdom have counterfeit power to intimidate and try to make God's people doubt and fear. But don't forget that the power of God far exceeds the counterfeit power of Satan.

The Holy Spirit will lead us to truth and repentance, but Satan will accuse us and try to lead us into feeling condemned. When we have a heart change, we will repent of sin and will be in the process of sanctification. The Holy Spirit sanctifies us and leads us into spiritual maturity. When we become mature Christians, we will not only recognize good, but we will recognize evil as well. According to Hebrews 5:14, a sign of spiritual maturity is discerning good from evil.

The power of the Holy Spirit will lead us to obedience. Through obedience the process of sanctification occurs, we are becoming more holy. The LORD has a special purpose and plan for our life. As we follow the leading of the Holy Spirit, we will become more and more obedient in walking out the plan He has for our life. The Word of God says in 2 Timothy 3:5, *"having a form of godliness but denying the power thereof: from such things turn away."* God gives us a spirit of power through the Holy Spirit. This power enables us to defeat Satan and all his lies. *"For God has not given us a spirit of fear, but of power and of love and of a sound mind"* (2 Timothy 1:7). His power is necessary in our lives for us to overcome and live an abundant life!

The Holy Spirit is our Helper, Comforter, Advocate, Intercessor, Counselor, Guide, Strengthener, and Standby. According to John 14:26, *"But the Helper, the Holy Spirit, whom the Father will send in My name (in My place, to represent me and act on My behalf), He will teach you all things. And He will help you remember everything that I have told you"*. The Holy Spirit will teach us all things. If we have a wounded soul, the Holy Spirit will empower and guide us into the truth that will heal our soul. The world's answer to our problems is to manage them, but the Holy Spirit wants to eliminate and remove the pain in our soul and heal us. We need to follow the Holy Spirit and obey Him to move into our healing. For example; if the Holy Spirit leads us to recognize unforgiveness we have towards someone, we need to obey the Holy Spirit to be healed and move into the abundant life God wants for us.

Who is leading you? Are you being led by fear or the Holy Spirit? If fear is the voice you are listening to, you will not find your peace or truth. If you are listening to the voice of fear, it will rush you and make you think you have to make decisions quickly. Satan pushes us to move quickly in hopes we don't hear the Holy Spirit guiding us, and we make a wrong decision. Be careful in making a permanent decision on a temporary problem (John 16:13).

According to John 15:26, the Holy Spirit is our Comforter. Is the Holy Spirit your Comforter or do you choose to go to something else for your comfort? Test yourself and examine where you go for your comfort. Is God the first thing you turn to or is it something or someone else?

God has a plan for our lives and work that He has planned for us to accomplish. The "anointing" of God is the power of God flowing through us to accomplish whatever He has assigned us to do. Without the power of the Holy Spirit, we will be doing work in our strength and will not have the ability or strength to accomplish the plans God has for us. *"Now to Him that is able to do exceeding abundantly above all that we ask or think, according to the power that works in us"* (Ephesians 3:20).

In Acts 10:38, God anointed Jesus with the Holy Spirit and with power (baptism of the Holy Spirit). Then Jesus went about healing the sick and setting the oppressed free. When God anoints us with the power of the Holy Spirit (baptism of the Holy Spirit), we will have the power to do what God has called us to do. According to Mark 16:17-18, *"And these signs shall follow them **that believe**; In My name shall they cast out devils; they shall speak with new tongues; They shall take up serpents; and if they drink any deadly thing, it shall not hurt them; they shall lay hands on the sick, and they shall recover."*

When Jesus sent His disciples out, they were sent out in groups of two. There is protection and strength when two or more people go out in ministry together. The Word of God says in Matthew 18:20 that where two or three are gathered together in the name of Jesus, He is present. When two or more are gathered to do God's work, they are stronger than if working alone. I can testify to the power of praying with a prayer partner. It is beautiful how the Holy Spirit will lead two or more people when they join together in His name. While one person may be praying, the other hears from the Holy Spirit regarding who or what to pray about next. It is like a beautifully orchestrated symphony where everyone's part is important for the symphony to work beautifully together.

The power of the Holy Spirit enables us to be overcomers in all aspects of our lives. The supernatural power given to us by the Holy Spirit will empower us to live a righteous life, fulfill the plans God has for our lives, strengthen us in trials, and enable us to resist temptations. The Holy Spirit that inhabits believers is healing to their body, mind, and soul. *"But if the Spirit of Him that raised up Jesus from the dead dwell in you, He that raised up Christ from the dead shall also quicken your mortal bodies by His Spirit that dwelleth in you"* (Romans 8:11).

When you are obedient to the leading of the Holy Spirit, the fruit of the Holy Spirit will be evident in your life. The characteristics or fruit of the Holy Spirit are love, joy, peace, patience, kindness, goodness, faithfulness, gentleness, and self-control (Galatians 5:22-26).

Those who are led by the Holy Spirit are the sons of God. If we follow our sinful desires, we can be led down the road to eternal death. Without the Holy Spirit leading us, we won't recognize the evil or have the strength to say no to it. *"For if you live after the flesh, you shall die: but if you through the Spirit do mortify the deeds of the body, you shall live. For as many as are led by the Spirit of God, they are the sons of God"* (Romans 8:13-14).

If we walk in the Spirit, we are not under the law. Under the law, we are not able to please God, but when we walk in the Spirit, we can walk in obedience because of His power working through us. When we are under the law, we are slaves. When we are slaves, we are using our efforts in life and trying to do right. I was a slave, and I never felt good enough. It was exhausting trying to strive in this life in my own efforts. Now I know the truth and my shackles are gone, and I am free in Christ. I am His daughter, and He will lead me as I humbly come before Him (Galatians 3:23-26).

When we are seeking God's direction in our life and making decisions, we want to wait on and listen to the Holy Spirit. We want to test whether what we are hearing is from God, Satan, the world, or ourselves. The following are some questions we can ask to test whether we are hearing from God:

1) God's voice will always line up with the Word of God.
2) God's voice will always line up with who God the Father is, who God the Son is, and who God the Holy Spirit is (1 John 5:7).
3) God's voice will go against the evil ways of the world.
4) God's voice will bring us peace that is not of this world (John 14:27).
5) God's direction will require courage and faith from us (Psalm 32:8-9, John 10:27).
6) God's voice will lead us, encourage us, comfort us, guide us, bring truth to us, convict us, but Satan's voice will lie to us, rush us, push us, frighten us, confuse us, discourage us, obsess us, and condemn us.

PERSONAL TESTIMONY: With the guidance of the Holy Spirit, I was led into an unexpected and beautiful friendship. If I had not listened to the Holy Spirit nudging me, I would have missed out on gaining the wisdom and insight God taught me through this friendship. Additionally, the friendship itself became a time of spiritual growth for both of us.

I somehow concluded, in my mind, that this neighbor had a very different personality than me, and we would probably never be friends. The Holy Spirit started nudging me to talk to her. Then one day, she told me her husband was very sick. I told her that God wanted her husband well and that her husband would be healed. My faith spoke boldly, and I told her to speak words of life in her home and over her husband. Her husband was healed!

The more we talked the closer our bond of friendship became. Our friendship began to blossom more when we began praying and studying the Bible together. Her family moved away, and we still remained faithful to our Bible study and prayers through the telephone and email. Later in our friendship, we were both going through similar trials, and we encouraged each other with the Word of God. Our friendship was so rich with the love of God. She became my sister in Christ, and this friendship will always hold a treasured place in my heart thanks to God and the work of the Holy Spirit.

CHAPTER 11

Satan and His Evil Kingdom

PERSONAL TESTIMONY

We don't wrestle with people; we wrestle with the kingdom of darkness. There was an evening where I was standing in such extreme fear because of an extremely difficult situation. This situation had gotten worse over a period of weeks. I was trying to sleep, and I felt an evil presence. This presence was trying to keep me from moving or speaking. I felt like I was being strangled with my blanket. There was no human being there. I knew something was extremely wrong so I kept trying to speak and call to Jesus, and I had to fight to speak any words out of my mouth. I was finally able to get up from my bed after struggling, and I knew my fear had to go. I knew that my fear had to be renounced. I had to walk in the strength of my Jesus who had defeated the enemy, and I had to agree with scripture that no power of the enemy could harm me! I had to make a very important decision that day; that I would agree with God's truth and renounce fear! Once I rebuked fear, this demonic presence had to leave. I had to speak in faith and take an act of faith (Luke 10:19, Ephesians 6:12).

OUR ENEMY: THE KINGDOM OF DARKNESS

God created heaven and earth. The sky above us, where the birds and clouds reside, can also be called the first heaven (Deuteronomy 11:17, Deuteronomy 28:12). The second heaven is where the planets, sun, moon, and stars are (Psalm 19:4, 6; Isaiah 13:10). <u>The third heaven is where God Almighty dwells</u> (2 Corinthians 12:2. Matthew 5:16).

There was war in heaven, and Satan was thrown out of heaven. *"And there was war in heaven: Michael and his angels fought against the dragon; and the dragon fought and his angels, and prevailed not; neither was their place found any more in heaven. And the great dragon was cast out, that old serpent, called the Devil, and Satan, which deceiveth the whole world: he was cast out into the earth, and his angels were cast out with him"* (Revelation 12:7-9).

Satan and his fallen angels have been cast out of heaven (Luke 10:18). Satan has lost his place in heaven, but he still has power and moves about the earth looking for who he can devour. *"Now there was a day when the sons of God came to present themselves before the LORD, and Satan also came among them. And the LORD said to Satan, "From where do you come?" So Satan answered the LORD and said, "From going to and fro on the earth, and from walking back and forth on it"* (Job 1:6-7). Satan and his evil kingdom set traps for all mankind and Satan accuses us day and night.

In Ephesians 6:11-12, it explains the levels of Satan's kingdom. Satan's kingdom is explained as principalities, powers, rulers of the darkness, and spiritual wickedness in high places.

Satan's goal is to torment us, keep us from knowing Christ, and keep us from completing the good work God prepared for us to do. *"For we are His workmanship, created in Christ Jesus to good works, which God has before ordained that we should walk in them"* (Ephesians 2:10).

Satan doesn't know how to tell the truth; he is the father of lies. Satan masquerades as an angel of light. His lies may look like the truth but don't be deceived, look underneath the mask. Satan will try to use people or circumstances to get you to believe his lies. Once you detect deception, seek and speak the truth from the Word of God (2 Corinthians 11:14).

TACTICS OF SATAN AND HIS EVIL KINGDOM

Freedom is of God. Bondage is of Satan (**FREEDOM**: <u>Galatians 5:1, Galatians 5:13, John 8:36</u>; **BONDAGE**: <u>2 Timothy 2:26, John 8:34, Acts 8:23</u>).

Don't give power to Satan by believing his lies. Adam and Eve agreed with the lies of Satan in the Garden and thus gave Satan permission to operate in their lives. Satan is a liar, and he tries to make us think God can't be trusted. Satan tries to redefine who God is and tries to get us to believe God isn't who He says He is (Genesis 3:2-24).

Satan will use partial truth from the Word of God and deceive us into believing it comes from God. He is the father of lies and is great at deception. Read Matthew 4:1-11 and see how Jesus spoke against Satan's lies. We can't be ignorant of Satan's devices. We don't want to be destroyed for lack of knowledge as written in Hosea 4:6.

We need to know our enemy, Satan, and his devices, so he does not cause us to stumble. Satan tries to deceive us and appear as light. Satan sets traps for us, and we need to be careful that he doesn't convince us that we can keep a "small sin" and think we can control it and put it away whenever we want (James 2:10).

God's word tells us we are not to fear. If we respond in fear, we give Satan power because we are agreeing with the kingdom of darkness. We are either agreeing with God's kingdom or Satan's kingdom, there is no in-between (1 John 4:18).

The fear that comes from the kingdom of darkness is a fear of torment. This fear is a spirit of fear and is of Satan. (See Chapter 5, The Author of Order where I describe the different types of fear.) Faith is of the spiritual realm and is of the Kingdom of Light. Faith is from God. Faith and the spirit of fear are both in the spiritual dimension but operate out of different kingdoms. When you fear something, you bring it into existence. When you have faith for something, you bring it into existence by your faith. You can test this out by finding someone who feared something long enough or stood in faith for something and then saw it manifest (Jeremiah 39:18).

Don't participate in allowing the devil to devour you by agreeing with his schemes and deception. According to 1 Peter 5:8, *"Be sober, be vigilant; because your adversary the devil, as a roaring lion, walketh about, seeking whom he may devour."* He walks around trying to drive fear into you. You need to be well-grounded by having the Word of God planted in your heart. Therefore, our foundation will be solid, and we will have the power of the Word of God to renounce the lies of Satan. Jesus is our example of overcoming Satan in our lives. Jesus overcame Satan when He was tempted in the wilderness. You can read about His victory in Matthew 4:1-11.

Beware of Satan's tactic of stealing the word from you immediately, after you have heard it. Mark 4:14-15, *"The sower soweth the word. And these are they by the way side, where the word is sown; but when they have heard Satan cometh immediately, and taketh away the word that was sown in their hearts."* Pray that the LORD protects the Word of God in your heart, and that His truth gets rooted in your heart.

Be careful what you look at, listen to, what you speak, what you believe, what you think, and your actions. When we listen to Satan, we fellowship with him. 1 Corinthians 10:20-21 says, *"But I say, that the things which the Gentiles sacrifice, they sacrifice to devils, and not to God: and I would not that you should have fellowship with devils. You cannot drink the cup of the LORD and the cup of devils; you cannot be partakers of the LORD's table and of the table of devils."*

Satan is trying to indoctrinate us and our children into his lies. We need to be careful about what we bring into our homes and what we are being exposed to outside our homes. We need to test whether we are idolizing anything in our home. Rebellion is of witchcraft; we should test the attitudes in our home. We should test whether there is strife or division in our home; where there is strife and division, the enemy can get a foothold. God should be the center of everything in our home. It is very important we spend time in our homes with the Word of God and talking about God. The more we talk in our families about what is truth; the more lies we can expose.

What we believe in our heart, whether good or evil, can change us for the better or for the worse. According to Proverbs 23:7, *"For as he thinketh in his heart, so is he: Eat and drink, saith he to thee; but his heart is not with thee."* Be wary of what beliefs are planted in your heart that are not the truth from God's word. For example: If you begin believing the lies someone said about you, you may start to have unloving thoughts about yourself. If this lie becomes true to you in your heart and then your soul is wounded, it can harm your body and soul. Be wary of these lies where Satan will work through people to hurt you. Stop agreeing with the venom Satan tries to poison you with.

PERSONAL TESTIMONY

During a very dark time of despair, I had this vision. I saw this white sterile-looking laboratory where there were ledges all around the various levels of the building. The kingdom of darkness would pull one family member, out at a time, on a ledge and try experiments on them. These experiments were deceptions and lies. Satan was waiting to see what lies or traps each family member would fall into. Satan plans to steal, kill, and destroy the family, but God plans to bring life and life more abundant. Once the enemies' lies are exposed and brought into the light, they begin to lose their power. I felt this vision was helping me understand and be aware that Satan was attacking my family. This vision helped me focus my attention on the spiritual aspect of our difficulties. It reminded me that my strength needed to go into spiritual warfare and that was where the battle was taking place. If I was putting my strength into the natural, I would not overcome because the battleground was in the spiritual realm. I understood little, if anything, about spiritual warfare but through difficulties it allowed God an opportunity to show me the battleground.

WARNING: SIN AND THE OPEN DOOR

If we come into agreement with sin (by agreeing with Satan and his evil kingdom), we open the door to the evil kingdom and open ourselves up to their evil. We are to hate Satan, demons, and sin. *"You that love the LORD, hate evil: He preserves the souls of His saints; He delivers them out of the hand of the wicked"* (Psalm 97:10).

Satan comes against us in our thought life. We need to resist his lies by casting off thoughts that are not godly. We will also need to cast off lies other people speak because Satan will use other people to get to us (2 Corinthians 10:5). According to Philippians 4:8, we are to focus our thoughts on those things that are true, honest, just, pure, lovely, good report, and praiseworthy.

When we believe Satan's lies and start speaking them, Satan has a stronghold in our life. Anything contrary to God's word is a lie. We don't want to develop an incorrect thinking pattern that agrees with Satan's lies. When we know the truth in the Word of God, we will destroy Satan's lies when we speak the truth.

Sinful acts can open the door to the demonic. The Word of God is very clear in identifying things of this world that can open the door to Satan and his evil kingdom. I have many scriptures in this paragraph identifying many of them. Take some time and study God's truth and evaluate your life for any potentially dangerous areas you may be deceived. (Ephesians 2:2, Isaiah 47:13-14, Deuteronomy 18:9-14, 1 Chronicles 10:13-14, 1 Samuel 28:1-25, Isaiah 8:19, Acts 16:16-19, Leviticus 20:6, Revelation 21:8, Leviticus 19:31, Leviticus 20:27, 1 John 4:1-4, 2 Kings 21:6, Exodus 20:1-17, Acts 13:6-8, 1 Timothy 4:1-3, Matthew 22:37-40, Isaiah 59:2, Proverbs 3:7, 1 Peter 5:8, Matthew 6:14-15, Ephesians 4:26-27, Matthew 18:21-35). Don't let Satan get you in his trapdoor of lies; be proactive and examine your life.

Satan will try to attack us when we have soul wounds. If our soul is wounded, we need to be delivered/healed from our soul wound. If there is a wounded soldier on the battlefield, they are more easily attacked by the enemy. When there is a wounded soul, it is more likely the wounded soul will listen to the flesh and not the spirit. Making wise decisions is less likely when our soul is wounded. Our soul can be wounded from sin, disobedience, a past hurt that was not dealt with, etc. With soul wounds, we can be entangled with unforgiveness, bitterness, hatred, rejection, rebellion, etc. These harmful things need to be removed from our soul.

These wounds can reside deep inside our soul, and we may not even realize that the wound remains. We can ask God to reveal to us any soul wounds we need to deal with. Once the soul wound is discovered, we can deal with it by recognizing our true feelings at the time it occurred; speak the truth from that experience; repent and forgive; and pray that through the power of Jesus's completed work on the cross, we are healed. Jesus Christ paid the debt for our iniquities and with His stripes, we are healed. The power of the Holy Spirit works through us to heal our soul. Recognizing how we were wounded guards us in the future from taking an offense because we have come to the knowledge of the truth. The truth sets people free. In John 4, Jesus spoke to the woman at the well. He spoke truth to her, about her sin, and that she had five husbands and the one she was with now was not her husband. Truth moves people out of their lies into the freedom that truth brings.

Another area for us to test is whether there is strife in our home. It is a good idea to have a strategy plan when problems arise in our home. It is beneficial to separate the person causing the strife from the rest of the family. These issues can grow like wildfire if not contained. Pray that God gives you wisdom in the situation. *"For where envy and self-seeking exist, confusion and every evil thing are there. But the wisdom that is from above is first pure, then peaceable, gentle, willing to yield, full of mercy and good fruits, without partiality and without hypocrisy"* (James 3:16-17). Be ready to protect your family with the Word of God and God's wisdom.

We will have temptation in this life, and we will be tested. Satan harasses mankind by tempting them to do evil and to destroy the work of God. In regards to being tested, metal is tested for its purity. God tests people to show their heart and thoughts. The way we handle the test will either glorify God or open the door to Satan. What opens the door to Satan? If we have disobeyed God, we have opened the door to Satan. When we agree with the lies of Satan, we open the door to the evil kingdom. That is why it is important to evaluate our beliefs and thoughts to judge whether they are of God or Satan, and therefore, determine who we are agreeing with (1 Peter 1:7).

Our words matter; they can bring life or death, blessing or a curse! Idle words are words that are careless or unprofitable words. We need to receive God's warning of speaking idle words. Words like "I'd be better off dead" or "I'm sick and tired" are careless words and Matthew 12:36-37 says they can condemn us. We will have to give an account of our idle words on judgment day. Additionally, Matthew 5:37 says, *"But let your 'yes' be 'yes' and your 'no' 'no'. For whatever is more than these is from the evil one."* We are to be truth speakers and truth seekers. If we are children of God, we are to speak the truth. We need to evaluate what comes out of our mouth. Are we lying because it is not acceptable to speak the truth according to the world's view? Are we lying to ourselves and then when we speak it is a lie? Are we lying to keep what we think is peace? Are we lying because we think we are protecting someone? We need to closely evaluate if we are speaking the truth in love. I believe the Holy Spirit will train us to speak the truth in love if we allow Him (Proverbs 6:2, Ecclesiastes 10:12-14).

Once you know who your enemy is and his tactics, our focus should then be on Christ. Don't be curious about the kingdom of darkness. We pay a very high price when we open the door to the demonic darkness and take a peek. The LORD tells us to stay away from such things as astrology, magic, mediums, divination, occult, and many more. It is very wise to research the origin or roots of a specific activity and not just blindly participate in any activity that the world offers. Many things are acceptable in our world but have no place with God. Some of these are yoga, Reiki healers, New Age, acupuncture, hypnotist, manipulation and domination which are of witchcraft, and many more. These things have crept into our world. Satan makes them look harmless, but they are not. Don't let Satan's subtleties deceive you. (Isaiah 47:13, Leviticus 20:6-27, Micah 3:7, Deuteronomy 18:9-12, Revelation 21:8, Jeremiah 27:9, Leviticus 19:31, Leviticus 19:26, 1 Chronicles 10:13, Isaiah 8:19, Exodus 7:11-22, Acts 16:16-18, Acts 19:19, Galatians 5:20-21, 2 Kings 23:24, 2 Kings 21:6, Matthew 11:28, Matthew 13:15, Ephesians 6:11-12).

JESUS OUR AUTHORITY

Satan accuses mankind day and night. Satan tells God that we are guilty of disobeying God's law continually. Because of Jesus's atonement, we as believers are not guilty. Therefore, Jesus disarmed the Satanic rulers and authorities. We are now justified. We now have the spiritual authority Jesus has given us to overcome the evil kingdom (Colossians 2:12-15).

Jesus came and destroyed the works of Satan. We will overcome by the blood of the Lamb and by the word of our testimony. What is your testimony of God's goodness and victory in your life? *"And they overcame him (Satan) by the blood of the Lamb, and by the word of their testimony; and they loved not their lives to the death"* (Revelation 12:11).

We are victorious through Christ who has won the battle over evil and brings us into His glorious light. *"Forasmuch then as the children are partakers of flesh and blood, He also Himself likewise took part of the same; that through death He might destroy him that had the power of death, that is, the devil; and deliver them who through fear of death were all their lifetime subject to bondage"* (Hebrews 2:14-15). Satan and his evil kingdom have been defeated by Jesus and the role of the church and believers is to appropriate it in our own life. *"Behold I give you the authority to trample on serpents and scorpions, and over all the power of the enemy, and nothing shall by any means hurt you"* (Luke 10:19).

We should search the scriptures like an attorney to prove our case against Satan's lies. Stand on the Word of God and His truth, not the accusations of Satan. We are enforcers of the truth! We need to first know the truth so we can enforce the truth and appropriate it in our own life (Revelation 12:9-13).

We need to repent of sin and forgive others so Satan does not gain a foothold. We disarm Satan by obeying God's commands. *"Now whom you forgive anything, I also forgive. For if indeed I have forgiven anything, I have forgiven that one for your sakes in the presence of Christ, lest Satan should take advantage of us; for we are not ignorant of his devices"* (2 Corinthians 2:10-11).

We can be deceived by Satan when our thoughts are led astray. Take every thought captive, don't allow your mind to continue in wrong thinking. If your thoughts are not bringing you peace, stop allowing your mind to move in that negative direction. Seek a scripture verse that will come against your wrong thinking pattern. Speak the Word of God out loud, instead of allowing your mind to continue down that pathway. It may seem hard at first to stop your wrong thinking but continue fighting your incorrect thinking with the Word of God, and you will defeat the lies. Speak out loud against the lie your thoughts are following. For example, saying out loud "I don't believe that lie, I am a child of God and I am more than a conqueror".

When you are faced with fear, you will either fight or flight. When Satan is coming at you with fear, fight against this by standing still and strong in the LORD and not turning your back to the enemy. When we flee evil, instead of renouncing and rebuking it, it chases us down. Fight the good fight of faith by coming against the evil with the Word of God, the blood of Jesus, and the power of the Holy Spirit.

The Sword of the Spirit is our offensive weapon against Satan. When we are fighting in the spirit realm, the spoken Word of God is our Sword of the Spirit. When Satan tempted Jesus, Jesus spoke words from scripture as His weapon and Satan left Him. Jesus knew the Word of God, and we need to be ready also to battle Satan with the Word of God. When we know the Word of God in our hearts, it flows out of our mouth (Ephesians 6:17, Luke 4:1-13).

Satan and his kingdom try to influence us, depress us, and oppress us. Therefore, we are to put on the whole armor of God and resist Satan. We need to agree with God and what God says about us and the victory we have. We are to enforce the victory Jesus won and appropriate it in our own life. We are overcomers and victorious through Jesus Christ and His redemptive work on the cross. But we must resist evil and submit to God (Ephesians 6:10-20).

Satan is the father of lies and comes to steal, kill, and destroy. We need to use God's word to kick Satan out of the places where he is trying to steal, kill, and destroy in our lives. Take inventory of the parts of your life where Satan may be trying to access. Kick Satan out of any place you have allowed entry; submit to God and resist Satan and he will flee. Here are some scripture verses declaring the completed work of Jesus Christ (Colossians 2:15, 1 John 4:4, 1 John 5:4, Revelation 12:11). Speak these verses out loud in faith. Satan is a liar, and he will try to convince you Jesus didn't defeat him. But Satan knows his time is short, and he will use many tactics to deceive. We need to proclaim, in faith, that Jesus was victorious over Satan and his evil kingdom.

Jesus, being full of the Holy Spirit, was led by the Holy Spirit into the wilderness where He encountered 40 days of conflict with Satan. After 40 days, Jesus was victorious over Satan. Jesus spoke the Word of God to defeat the lies of Satan. After this victory, Jesus started His public ministry "in the power of the Spirit". We as Jesus's disciples will have to encounter evil and overcome. Jesus came out of this spiritual battle "in the power of the Spirit". We need to have the Word of God planted in our heart so we are prepared and ready to defeat Satan when he comes.

Part of Jesus's ministry was casting out demons. In the name of Jesus Christ, we have spiritual authority over the power of the kingdom of darkness. We have the spiritual authority to resist the devil, and he will flee. We are the church, and the church has the spiritual authority to cast out demons (2 Corinthians 10:3-5, James 4:7-10, Mark 16:16-18).

PERSONAL TESTIMONY

I did yoga for years and never researched its origin. It was widely accepted in society, and I never thought too much about the roots of yoga. There was even a Christian church that I attended and one evening a week they had someone teach yoga and read scripture as we did yoga. I was teaching at an elementary school where they practiced yoga in the special education classes. They used yoga as a calming technique for the students.

I have been warned by several teachers/pastors that yoga is an occult. As I researched the origin of yoga, I found it began 5000 years ago from India. The word "yoga" originated from India's oldest sacred writings called Rig Veda. These Veda writings were songs and rituals used by the Vedic priests. Out of these ancient writings began Buddhism and Hinduism.

There is a yoga pose called "Savasana" which is also known as "corpse pose". There is also a yoga pose called "Cobra pose". I have realized how important it is to research the origin of everything we do, and not just engage in an activity because it is popular in society. I never practiced Kundalini Yoga, but as I researched yoga, I found Kundalini yoga was described as "manifesting the power of our inner serpent". No matter what the yoga is called it all has an origin in a dark spiritual place with roots of an occult. The Word of God warns us about divination and occult practices (1 Samuel 15:23, Deuteronomy 18:9-14).

When things become commonplace in our society, we need to be wary and alert about potential pitfalls. I am very thankful my eyes have been opened to the truth about yoga. I stopped practicing yoga immediately and repented. Many other things in our society are not acceptable to God. If you are unsure whether something is God-pleasing, seek scripture for truth and simply ask God to reveal the truth to you. God has laws and commands that never change in His word. He is trying to protect us from evil.

CHAPTER 12

Don't Be Deceived

The love of our Heavenly Father is different from the love the world offers. I feel the LORD has shown me His immense love for me by showing me how not to be deceived. I am sharing this chapter with you because I want you to be alert too. I was not completely aware of the battleground.

DON'T BE DECEIVED: Maybe you don't see people worshipping golden calves or stirring up a witches brew, but don't be deceived, there are occult activities and idolatry quite evident in the United States. Don't let the subtlety of the world deceive you. When you don't practice your spiritual discernment, you can become numb to the deception in the world. Today the lies of the world and the lies of Satan come in subtly, especially if you are not practicing your spiritual discernment. It is important to be alert so you are not deceived. There are witches, warlocks, sorcery, and image worship present in our world and nation. People are practicing outright witchcraft with spells, and then there are more subtle forms of witchcraft by which people manipulate, control, and intimidate others to control some future event. Another example of witches, warlocks, and sorcerers, in our culture, is fantasy video games or role playing games. Some people practice being a witch, warlock, or sorcerer for many hours a day in a fantasy role. God has given us our imaginations for good but Satan has deceived us into using our imaginations for evil (Galatians 5:19-21).

DON'T BE DECEIVED: Idolatry is image worship. Idol worship is more than just a golden calf. Most of the idolatry of today may be more subtle like idolizing yourself, or another person, possibly a sportsperson or celebrity, or idolizing an object in your home that you put in very high value. There are many pagan and false gods today in many different forms. Some examples are money, power, status, physical appearance, pleasure, food, religious tradition, and political or social change. When you put your value in these things above God, this is idolatry. God knows the heart of a man. According to Bible Study Tools, <u>idolatry</u> is defined as "image-worship or divine honor paid to any created object". Thayers Greek Lexicon defines <u>idolatry</u> as "the worship of false gods". In today's world, when people look to God for what they want from God instead of their relationship with God, they are idolizing what God can do for them above God Himself. We are to seek God to have a relationship with Him not what He can give us. Others turn their relationship with God into their personalized god to meet their needs and what they desire God to be. We have to be careful we aren't deceived in our thoughts to make things more comfortable for ourselves by believing the lies in our head or from Satan, of who God is. God is who He says He is. We are made in God's image and are not made to worship images but to worship God (Genesis 1:27, Galatians 5:20-21).

DON'T BE DECEIVED: God does not control or intimidate us to manipulate our free will. Manipulation is defined as "to control or play upon by artful, unfair, or insidious means especially to one's own advantage" (from Merriam-Webster). Don't let subtle manipulative behavior begin to start a pattern that escalates. When we feed bad behavior, it grows. God gives us free will, and we have freedom in Christ. Expose any behavior that is manipulating your free will; speak up and let the person know what they are doing because they may not even be aware.

I met a mom who told me her story. When she was quite young, her older brother using control and intimidation drove her to get an abortion. The controlling and intimidating nature of this led her to feel she didn't even have a choice in this matter. Manipulation and intimidation are of witchcraft; witchcraft is a desire to know the future and control events that are not ours to control. Witchcraft can be subtle, where someone isn't even aware they are doing it. That is why it is important to expose it by making the person aware of their action. Manipulating the spirit realm to get what you want whether it is knowingly or unknowingly is witchcraft. Satan and his evil kingdom teach these evil practices (1 King 21).

DON'T BE DECEIVED: According to BibleStudy.org, the occult is "any practice that tries to gain supernatural power, abilities, or knowledge apart from the creator God". According to Dictionary.com, the definition of occult is "of or relating to magic, astrology, or any system claiming use or knowledge of secret or supernatural power or agencies". The act of witchcraft is an occult activity and is the desire to know the future and control events that are not ours to control. These abilities belong to God only. In Genesis 3:5, Satan said to Eve, "you can be like God". We are to be free of fear and trust God for our future and flee from occult activity of any kind. Don't let anyone deceive you and tell you the following things are harmless. Warning! keep away from: horoscopes, astrology, fortune-telling, hypnotism, tarot cards, psychics, Ouija boards, ESP, necromancy, Wicca, Reiki, magic, statues of idols, mind control, rebellion, palm reading, rituals, yoga, role-playing games, acupuncture, casting spells, consulting mediums, taking a substance to achieve an altered state of consciousness, charms, dominating or controlling people to manipulate their free will, etc. We need to be aware of the things in our society that draw us into this evil. There are signs of evil activity if you will look for them. For instance, I was in an unfamiliar department store, and I felt a strange evil presence that I couldn't explain. I started examining the clothing and noticed that the clothing was all light and pretty colors but the symbols on the clothing were Satanic. One t-shirt had what looked like a lemonade stand with little children on the shirt. As I further examined the shirt, there was a small sign on the lemonade stand that said: "sell your soul". We need to be careful of what items we bring into our homes and where they come from. God says do not be afraid, but He also says don't be ignorant of the enemy's devices (Leviticus 20:27, 1 Chronicles 10:13, 2 Chronicles 33:6).

DON'T BE DECEIVED: There are people who worship Satan in the United States, and there are witches and warlocks. It is not something in a far off land. There are people who sacrifice to Satan in the United States. When I lived in Arizona, I met a young lady who I ministered to at a homeless women's ministry. She had grown up in the Midwest in a pagan lifestyle as a child. Her parents practiced witchcraft. When I met her, she had some very unusual sicknesses and mental torment because of the occult life she was raised in. She fled 2,000 miles, away from her parents, to escape the occult life of her parents (Deuteronomy 18:10-14, Isaiah 47:8-14).

DON'T BE DECEIVED: Not only is there a heaven, but there is a hell where there will be eternal torment for the unsaved. *"This is all the more urgent, for you know how late it is; time is running out. Wake up, for our salvation is nearer now than when we first believed. The night is almost gone; the day of salvation will soon be here. So remove your dark deeds like dirty clothes, and put on the shining armor of right living* *because we belong to the day, we must live decent lives for all to see. Don't participate in the darkness of wild parties and drunkenness, or in sexual promiscuity and immoral living, or in quarreling and jealousy. Instead, clothe yourself with the presence of the LORD Jesus Christ, and don't let yourself think about ways to indulge your evil desires"* (Romans 13:11-14). Satan is not in hell yet. He is roaming about seeing who he can devour (1 Peter 5:8).

DON'T BE DECEIVED: We are to obey the will of the Father. According to Matthew 7:21, *"Not everyone that saith unto me, LORD, LORD shall enter into the kingdom of heaven; but he that doeth the will of my Father which is in heaven."* We all need to test ourselves; are we obeying the Word of God, are we sorrowfully repenting, are we forgiving others? (Revelation 22:14-15)

DON'T BE DECEIVED: After you are saved, you are not promised an easy life here on earth but *"work out your own salvation with fear and trembling"* (Philippians 2:12). When you are working out at the gym, you are exercising to stay in shape. Don't become lazy after you are saved. You will need to exercise your faith, practice self-control, and discipline yourself. God has given you a spirit of power, love, and sound mind.

DON'T BE DECEIVED: Follow God and His word, not man. We are all subject to error because we are human, but God never lies and is always the truth giver. Therefore, always verify anything you hear or read with the Word of God. Even our own thoughts can lead us astray from God and His truth. Examine your thoughts against the Word of God (2 Peter 2:1-3, 1 John 4:1).

DON'T BE DECEIVED: In Revelation 2:20 the LORD says, *"Nevertheless I have a few things against you, because you allow that woman Jezebel, who calls herself a prophetess, to teach and seduce My servants to commit sexual immorality and eat things sacrificed to idols."* What are we allowing to continue that God is calling us to confront? We are not told to tolerate evil and sin in our lives.

DON'T BE DECEIVED: Stubbornness and pride can really be a stumbling block to the truth. When we put up a wall and think we already know everything about God and His truth, how can we hear from the Holy Spirit and have revelation. ". . . Stubbornness is as iniquity and idolatry . . ." (1 Samuel 15:23)

DON'T BE DECEIVED: According to Revelation 13:16-18, we are told about the mark of the beast. There will come a time when all people will have to have the mark of the beast (false prophet, antichrist) to be able to buy or sell. The number of the beast is 666. The mark will be placed either on the forehead or the right hand to indicate the followers of the antichrist. From the Strong's Concordance (Greek, Hebrew), the word "mark" means stamp, scratch or etching. It is becoming more commonplace for many to get markings on their bodies. We want to be careful we are not indoctrinated by Satan and drawn into his deception in this area.

DON'T BE DECEIVED: In Joshua 24, verse 15, we are told to choose this day who we will serve. Are we serving God, ourselves, the world, Satan, an idol, a lie? If we are serving a lie (which is believing a lie and thus in bondage to the lie), Satan may convince us to be strong and courageous for something that is actually a lie. Aren't we suppose to be strong and courageous for truth? To serve truth, we must know truth.

DON'T BE DECEIVED: According to 2 Corinthians 13:5, we need to test ourselves to see if we are in the faith. Don't let Satan gain a foothold in your life. Test yourself to make sure you are in the faith. Some questions to test yourself: Where is my relationship with God? What is the condition of my heart towards God and others? Am I reading the Word of God and obeying? Is the noise of the world so loud that I can't hear God? (1 John 3:9, Hebrews 10:26)

"Behold I stand at the door, and knock: if any man hear My voice, and open the door, I will come in to him, and will sup with him, and he with Me" (Revelation 3:20). Why don't you invite the LORD in to sit at the table with you and talk to Him about whatever is on your heart and mind? He wants to be invited into your everyday. This will be the most important invitation you will ever send! He is standing at the door, knocking. Will you let Him in?

CHAPTER 13
Spiritual Roots

In our culture today, searching for our ancestral family history and DNA is very popular. I wonder how many people have actually given any thought to their spiritual roots in their family tree and the reason bad fruit was produced? Colossians 2:6-7 says, *"As you have therefore received Christ Jesus the LORD, so walk you in Him: Rooted and built up in Him, and established in the faith, as you have been taught, abounding therein with thanksgiving."* This verse speaks of the good roots grounded in Jesus Christ, and this will produce good fruit. But there are bad spiritual roots that can creep into our family tree or in our own life that produce bad fruit. Some examples of bad spiritual roots would be unforgiveness (towards self, God, or another person), idolatry, bitterness, pride, hatred, envy and jealousy, and occultism (witchcraft and divination). According to 1 Samuel 15:23, the root of stubbornness is idolatry, and the root of rebellion is witchcraft.

What does the medical field say about unforgiveness and unhealthy emotions? John Hopkins Medicine has published an article called <u>Forgiveness: Your Health Depends on It</u>. It states that being hurt and disappointed has an enormous impact on our body. It states chronic anger puts you into a fight or flight mode and results in changes in heart rate, blood pressure, and the immune response. It indicates how when you forgive there are many health benefits. Additionally, an article called <u>Forgiveness: Letting Go of Grudges and Bitterness,</u> by Mayo Foundation for Medical Education and Research, states that forgiving someone can lead to healthier relationships, improved mental health, less anxiety, lower blood pressure, fewer symptoms of depression, stronger immune system, improved heart health, and improved self-esteem. Additionally, there is an article from CBN News called <u>The Deadly Consequences of Unforgiveness</u> by Lori Johnson. In this article, Dr. Steven Standiford, Chief of Surgery from Cancer Treatment Centers of America, states that refusing to forgive others makes people sick and keeps them sick. From this same article, Dr. Michael Barry, a pastor, and author of the book <u>The Forgiveness Project</u> states that 61 percent of cancer patients have problems with forgiving others. He indicates half of them have severe forgiveness issues.

Now that we have taken a look at what the medical field says about forgiveness and negative emotions, let's look at what fruit your family tree is producing. When a family tree has bad fruit, we should examine what spiritual root is causing the family to produce the bad fruit. God wants us to produce good fruit, and when we examine ourselves and our family, we will be able to recognize the familiar problems and remove them.

God designed the family unit and Satan wants to destroy the family unit. Satan wants to bring curses into the family tree to cause vicious cycles and keep the whole family in bondage. God created the family to be united and to have a father and a mother; whereby, the father is the head of the household. The love in a family is to bear all things, to rejoice in the truth, is patient and kind, does not envy, is not arrogant, is not resentful, and endures all things. When the family is out of God's order, deterioration occurs because it is not the Master Designer's plan.

We need to evaluate ourselves and our ancestors and the fruit we produce. We can research our family tree and document any repetitive bad fruit. Examples of bad fruit could be addictions, illnesses, legal trouble, poverty, mental illness, etc. If we are finding repeated patterns of bad fruit in our family tree, the next step is to determine the spiritual root. Sometimes when you talk to family members you may find that various people in the family may struggle with forgiving others, and unforgiveness can cause all kinds of bad fruit. Some other examples from the Word of God are witchcraft (occult) and idolatry. The Word of God says if there is rebellion, it is rooted in witchcraft. When someone in the family is manipulating, controlling, intimidating, or dominating someone's free will, this is witchcraft. Furthermore, it states that stubbornness is rooted in idolatry; whereby, the person believes their opinion or judgment is above all others.

In Nehemiah 9:1-3, the children of Israel came together with fasting and prayer and confessed their sin and the iniquities of their fathers. God wants us to recognize our sin and iniquity that has gone on for generations. He wants us to make a course correction if we are headed down the wrong road.

Repeated patterns of bad fruit, within the family tree, are a warning sign. The generational iniquity needs to be pulled out at the root by repentance, obedience, and making a course adjustment by agreeing with truth.

First of all, once your research is completed into your family tree, you can analyze what you assess the common bad fruit is and determine the spiritual root. For example, if there is a pattern of anxiety and panic attacks, the spiritual root could be fear. Further research may be needed into what type of fear it is; fear of man, fear of failure, fear of the future, etc. The whole purpose of finding the spiritual root is to expose it. When you bring darkness into the light, it loses its power. **Second**, rebuke and renounce the iniquity (spiritual root). Thus, you are no longer agreeing with this evil. **Third**, repent (sorrowfully) on behalf of your involvement and on behalf of your family's sin and iniquity within your generations (name the evil spiritual root that was unveiled). It would be extremely beneficial if you can gather the family together and humbly come before God and repent, similar to what the children of Israel did in Nehemiah 9:1-3. **Fourth**, using your spiritual authority as a believer in Jesus Christ, name the iniquity (spiritual root) that was unveiled in your family and agree that the curse was broken off according to Galatians 3:13-15. **Fifth,** now come into agreement with the Word of God that counters the lies of Satan regarding the spiritual root that was found. For example, if the spiritual root was fear, search scripture for verses on faith Faith comes by hearing; therefore, read the scriptures out loud. **Lastly**, pray to remove all incorrect thinking patterns and agreements that led to this iniquity (spiritual root), and ask God to reveal the next step for you and your family and their wholeness (Isaiah 58). There will be actions you need to take that will reveal your faith and move you into your freedom. Therefore, Satan will lose his power over you and your family. Fight for freedom for your children and yourself. Our bloodlines can be transformed by faith like Abraham. Our faith in God's truth has no expiration date. Abraham never saw the Promised Land but his seed did.

A really good resource to help you with removing and understanding spiritual roots is Dr. Henry Wright. He has books, teachings on CD, and some YouTube teachings. Below are some scripture verses you can study for further understanding: John 15:4, Luke 6:43-45, Galatians 5:16-26, Hebrews 12:15, Matthew 3:10, Ephesians 3:16-19, Numbers 14:18, Exodus 20:5, and Proverbs 26:2.

CHAPTER 14
Our Spiritual Authority Through Jesus Christ

God said to man in Genesis be fruitful and multiply, fill the earth and subdue it, and have dominion over every living thing. The LORD has given the earth to men, and we have authority on the earth. We are a chosen people and a royal priesthood. We are called to walk in our dominion on the earth and bring God's kingdom to earth. We have dominion over the earth which includes dominion over the work of Satan's evil kingdom. Are we going to use our dominion and spiritual authority as believers and fight for our victory and overcome Satan in our own lives? *"The heaven, even the heavens, are the LORD's: but the earth has He given to the children of men"* (Psalm 115:16). (Genesis 1:28)

We are daughters and sons of the King. The King has given us spiritual authority on earth and our words have the power to bring life or death, blessing or cursing. We need to be careful with our words. We are accountable to God for our words. We are spirit beings, and we speak things into the future with our words. In the spirit realm, both faith and fear produce results. Our faith-filled words move mountains. Our fear-filled words produce unfavorable outcomes from our words and actions. *"A man shall eat good by the fruit of his mouth: but the soul of the transgressors shall eat violence. He that keeps his mouth keeps his life: but he that opens wide his lips shall have destruction"* (Proverbs 13:2-3). Additionally, Matthew 12:36-37 says, *"But I say to you, that every idle word that men shall speak, they shall give account thereof in the day of judgment. For by your words you shall be justified, and by your words you shall be condemned."* These two texts of scripture detail the seriousness of our words and how we can speak word curses over our own lives by the careless words we speak. We want to make sure our words are bringing life, not death.

We were created in God's image. God spoke things into being with His words. Therefore, we shall decree something, and it will be established. When we follow the LORD with all our heart, what we decree and declare will stand because we are walking in truth and faith. What we speak with our mouth and believe in our heart will come to pass. We shall speak things that are not, as though they were. *"You shall decree a thing, and it shall be established to you: and the light shall shine upon your ways"* (Job 22:28). What are you believing in your heart and professing with your mouth; is it faith or fear? How are you using your spiritual authority? (Romans 4:17, Romans 10:9-13)

Are you an overcomer? An overcomer prevails and is victorious. Jesus has won the battle over Satan. Therefore, as believers, we are to enforce this victory in our own lives. We are overcomers: when we believe Jesus is the Son of God and rose again; when we walk by faith not by sight; when we are obedient to our Heavenly Father; when we bring heaven to earth; and when we overcome evil in our own lives. *"You are of God, little children, and have overcome them: because greater is He that is in you, than he (Satan) that is in the world"* (1 John 4:4).

OUR SPIRITUAL AUTHORITY: VICTORIOUS THROUGH JESUS CHRIST

Jesus came to destroy the works of Satan. *"He that commits sin is of the devil; for the devil sinned from the beginning. For this purpose the Son of God was manifested, that He might destroy the works of the devil"* (1 John 3:8). Jesus destroyed the works of Satan when He lived a sinless life, died on the cross, and was resurrected. *"For Christ also has once suffered for sins, the just for the unjust, that He might bring us to God, being put to death in the flesh, but quickened (made alive) by the Spirit"* (1 Peter 3:18). Jesus conquered sin and Satan by His sinless life, death on the cross, and His resurrection; His finished work on the cross. *"And they said, believe on the LORD Jesus Christ and you shall be saved and your house"* (Acts 16:31). As God's children, we are overcomers because greater is He that is in us than he (Satan) that is in the world (1 John 4:4). Through Jesus Christ, we are victorious and overcomers, we need to use the authority Jesus gained over Satan by His death and resurrection. We are children of God through our faith in Jesus Christ as our LORD and Savior. According to Matthew 28:18-20 and Mark 16:15-19, Jesus gave His authority to His disciples before He ascended into heaven. Jesus won the victory over sin, Satan, the curse of the law, and death, and we now fight the good fight of faith. Jesus is our example of overcoming. *"And they overcame him by the blood of the Lamb, and by the word of their testimony; and they loved not their lives unto the death"* (Revelation 12:11). We are victorious through the blood of Jesus Christ and the words of our testimony.

OUR SPIRITUAL AUTHORITY AS BELIEVERS, AND THE CHURCH

As disciples of Jesus Christ, we are called to share Jesus with the lost, baptize those who believe, lay hands on the sick, stand against Satan and sin, cast out demons, raise the dead, and fulfill the plan God has for our life. As the LORD's disciples, He has plans for our lives that He has planned for us to do. *"For we are His workmanship, created in Christ Jesus for good works, which God prepared beforehand that we should walk in them"* (Ephesians 2:10). (Mark 16:15-18)

As disciples, we are to enforce God's truth and resist Satan. We resist Satan by submitting to God. We are to appropriate Jesus's victory into our own lives. Jesus gave His church power over evil. We need to know how to use our spiritual authority and agree with the victory Jesus already won over evil. Jesus used the Word of God when He was tempted in the desert. Jesus came out of the desert with the "power of the Holy Spirit". We are to overcome as Jesus did with the Word of God and faith (Revelation 12:9-12).

God's Church is the only hope for many of the battles raging in the world today. God is very clear in the Word of God on marriage, the unborn baby, loving God, loving ourselves, and loving fellow man. If the Church is lukewarm on any of these, how is the unbelieving world going to see God on the earth. We are to bring His kingdom to earth (Revelation 3:16, 2 Timothy 4:3-4).

Peter used his spiritual authority over Satan when he met a lame beggar. Then Peter said, *"Silver and gold I do not have, but what I do have I give you: In the name of Jesus Christ of Nazareth, rise up and walk* (Acts 3:6)". Peter used his spiritual authority in the name of Jesus. The lame beggar was healed and the infirmity left him. If we are passive and not using our spiritual authority, we will miss helping ourselves and others. We need to be fighting forcefully against the kingdom of darkness to enforce Jesus's victory in our own lives and helping others to be set free (Luke 10:19).

Who or what are you agreeing with? And who or what are you submitting to? Are you agreeing with what the world says and submitting to the world's ways or are you agreeing with what the Word of God says and submitting to God? The Word of God is very specific as to what is true and acceptable to the LORD. We need to be careful we are not twisting what the Word of God says to make things easier on ourselves. Satan will lie to us to attempt to deceive us about the truth of the Word of God. Satan's ways are very devious, and we need to be extremely careful we don't go astray with false teachings or lies. Satan is the father of lies, and we need to evaluate our beliefs against the Word of God for ourselves and not always take someone else's word for it.

God is a God who gives us choices. He created us with a mind and heart to make choices. Our minds need to be renewed and our hearts kept pure. We want to make choices that please God and not follow our own desires which can lead us astray. Adam and Eve were given many trees in the Garden of Eden to eat. They were told the only tree they could not eat was the tree of the knowledge of good and evil. The authority God gave Adam and Eve, Adam and Eve turned over to Satan when they listened to his lie and submitted to Satan (Genesis 3). When Jesus came to earth and overcame sin and Satan by His sinless life, death, and resurrection; He destroyed the works of Satan for those that believe. Now we need to stand on our authority and claim God's truth, not Satan's lies. We have been given the ability to choose which side we believe: the Kingdom of Light or the kingdom of darkness. There is no middle ground (Hebrews 2:14-18, Psalm 115:16).

Satan gains authority in our lives when we sin and believe his lies. When Satan convinces us that he has not been defeated, he gains authority in our lives and will trespass in our lives. Satan will trespass until we force him out with the Word of God and our faith. Satan can build a stronghold (incorrect thinking pattern) in our minds where we believe lies that can get us spiritually stuck in the mud. Pray that the LORD reveals any lies to you and reveals the truth. We need to seek God and know His Word, and His truth will defeat Satan (2 Corinthians 11:3).

Whatever you submit to and agree with becomes your master. If you are submitting and agreeing with fear, fear is now your master. Stand up to your fear and say "you are no longer welcome here, I kick you out. I trust God, and fear you are a liar and you must leave!!" *"For you have not received the spirit of bondage again to fear; but you have received the spirit of adoption, whereby we cry Abba Father"* (Romans 8:15). Repent before the LORD of living in fear and turn from fear, stand in faith, and walk in God's peace (Matthew 6:24).

What you agree with has dominion over you! *"For sin will no longer be a master over you, since you are not under Law (as slaves), but under (unmerited) grace (as recipients of God's favor and mercy). What then (are we to conclude)? Shall we sin because we are not under Law, but under (God's) grace? Certainly not! Do you not know that when you continually offer yourselves to someone to do his will, you are the slaves of the one whom you obey, either (slaves) of sin, which leads to death, or of obedience, which leads to righteousness (right standing with God)?"* (Romans 6:14-16). When we agree with God's will for our life, and therefore are obedient, we have freedom and are not in bondage to the lies of Satan.

Satan and his evil kingdom will try to steal from you and your family, he will try to kill you and your family, and he will try to destroy you and your family. Don't let him!! I did not understand these things. The truth has set me free, and I now know how to fight the good fight of faith. Once you know the truth and God has given you revelation, you want to help others receive their freedom. That is why I am writing down the truths I learned because I was transformed, and I never want to go back to my prior way of living in darkness. I want others that are living in darkness to be set free and know the truth (John 10:10, John 8:43-47).

We have spiritual authority over sickness. Jesus paid the price for all sin, sickness, and curses on the cross. Our Healer, Jehovah-Rapha, wants all our diseases healed. Exodus 15:26 states "... *I am the LORD that healeth thee.*" The LORD is the Healer and wants you healed. When Jesus ascended into heaven, He commissioned His disciples to heal the sick. *"Is any sick among you? Let him call for the elders of the church; and let them pray over him, anointing him with oil in the name of the LORD: and the prayer of faith shall save (heal) the sick, and the LORD shall raise him up; and if he have committed sins, they shall be forgiven him"* (James 5:14-15). There are many verses of scripture on healing. We, as believers of Jesus Christ, are to appropriate this truth in our own lives. We are to enforce that Jesus is the Healer and wants you healed!

God has given us the choice of life or death, blessings or curses, obedience or disobedience. We choose whose side we are on, the Kingdom of Light or the kingdom of darkness. Our words and actions reveal what we have chosen. The war we are in is between good and evil; not a war between two political parties, or between people. It is a spiritual war of good and evil that stirs up all kinds of trouble across the globe and arguments in our own living room. We are in a battle between the Kingdom of Light and the kingdom of darkness. Many people have no idea that the real battle is spiritual, not a battle between races or political parties. Our battle is fought and won in prayer and by our spiritual authority and spiritual warfare, not arguments (Deuteronomy 30:15-20, James 4:7-10).

We are in the good fight of faith. There is no middle ground with God; we are either on God's side or Satan's side. We are taking sides by our choices, our words, our time, etc. God's disciples don't sit on the sidelines; there is an assignment He has given to each of us. We need to find what our assignment is and put our heart completely into it. His plan for our life will give us more joy than anything in this world.

OUR SPIRITUAL AUTHORITY: OUR WORDS AND ACTIONS

Every word we speak and every word we hear either administers life or death. In the spirit realm, our words bring forth life or death. We need to be mindful of what we are listening to since these words affect our soul. We will be accountable for our careless words (idle words) we speak. We are spirit beings and our words have a powerful impact in the spirit realm. *"But I say to you that for every idle word men may speak, they will give account of it in the day of judgment"* (Matthew 12:36). *"Death and life are in the power of the tongue, and those who love it will eat its fruit"* (Proverbs 18:21). We need to be careful with our words, and this is very serious to the LORD. There is power in our words; we speak either life or death with our words. We need to allow the Holy Spirit to speak to us and give us His guidance before we just speak the first thing that comes to our thoughts. A beautiful example of allowing the Holy Spirit to speak through us is the Margie Mayfield testimony which you can find on Youtube.com. This YouTube video is the testimony of Margie Mayfield's encounter with serial killer Stephen Morin and his conversion. Margie waited on the Holy Spirit as she spoke to Stephen Morin who abducted her. Stephen ended up giving his life to Christ as a result of this. It is an extremely powerful story of waiting on the Holy Spirit and the powerful testimony that resulted (Luke 12:12).

We have spiritual authority over words spoken against us. *"No weapon formed against you shall prosper, and every tongue which rises against you in judgment you shall condemn. This is the heritage of the servants of the LORD, and their righteousness is from Me,"* says the LORD (Isaiah 54:17). We need to counter-attack any negative words against us. We must speak against any words that were spoken to harm us. For example: If someone says to you, "You look like you are dying." You could say, "No, I am full of life." Our words have power, and we are told to condemn the words against us. Our words bring life and death; and if someone speaks death with their words towards you, you can speak life and not agree with their words of death (Proverbs 18:21). We are not to argue or accuse but to speak the truth in love. The Word of God says to cast down arguments. *"Casting down arguments and every high thing that exalts itself against the knowledge of God, bringing every thought into captivity to the obedience of Christ"* (2 Corinthians 10:5).

When we speak life, we produce the fruit of life! We reap what we sow. When we speak life with our words, we bless ourselves and those around us. We can speak healing into existence by our words of faith. When we speak in faith the Word of God, it brings forth life. When we prophesy over our life or make a declaration, we need to believe in our heart what we are saying (Galatians 6:7, Psalm 89:34).

We are to call things that are not, as though they were. We are to speak life into our lives and others by the words we speak. We are made in God's image, and this is what God did, and we are to follow His example. We need to speak by faith calling things that are not, as though they are. When we believe, we see the glory of God (John 11:40, Romans 4:17, 2 Corinthians 4:13).

We all have a choice of blessing or cursing, life or death. *"I call heaven and earth as witnesses today against you, that I have set before you life and death, blessing and cursing: therefore choose life, that both you and your descendants may live"* (Deuteronomy 30:19). Choose blessings and life! Take special notice that in Deuteronomy 30:19 that our choices affect our descendants and their life. Our choices have consequences. What we allow in our homes affects our family, and what we speak affects our family. We have authority in our home to speak blessings over our family. Prophesy is a declaration of the future. Since we have authority in our own households and our words have the power of life or death, we should be speaking life over our children and spouses. We need to declare blessings over their futures and be using the authority God has given us for their good (Ezekiel 37:4-6, Proverbs 18:21, Deuteronomy 28:15-68).

We are to decree things by speaking God's kingdom here on earth. We are seated with Christ in the heavenly realm. We need to use the authority God has given us to bring heaven to earth. We are to make declarations, and they will be established. It is very powerful what we believe in our heart and then speak with our lips. According to Job 22:21-29, we are to come humbly to God, remove iniquity from our heart, and abide with the LORD. Then when we make declarations for ourselves and our family, they will manifest because we were obedient to God and believed in our heart.

PERSONAL TESTIMONY: THE POWER IN OUR WORDS

A few years ago, I was a substitute teacher in a 2nd grade classroom. There was a student in the back row who kept his head down, on his desk, during class. I went to the back of the class to ask him to sit up. He didn't respond. The students told me he falls asleep all the time in class and has trouble waking up and staying awake. The students told me to just leave him alone because he always sleeps in the classroom. Then his mother came into the classroom and was trying to wake him up to do work. I was told his mother comes in the classroom often to assist her son. The students told me the boy's name was "Sleep". What was so amazing was that I had just been studying the power of our words and that the Word of God says that death and life are in the power of the tongue. This child hears his name over and over again, "Sleep, Sleep!" Our words matter more than we realize!!

OUR SPIRITUAL AUTHORITY: THE WORD OF GOD

Jesus was tempted by Satan in the wilderness. Jesus used the Word of God to overcome Satan's lies. We, likewise, will need to overcome Satan's lies with the Sword of the Spirit (Word of God). We need to know scripture and have it planted in our hearts. When Satan tempts us, we will then be ready to fight with the Sword of the Spirit (Word of God) as Jesus did. According to Matthew 4:10, *"Then Jesus said to him, Away with you, Satan! For it is written, 'You shall worship the LORD your God, and Him only you shall serve.'"* According to Matthew 4:4, *"But He answered and said, 'It is written man shall not live by bread alone, but by every word that proceeds from the mouth of God.'"* The Word of God is our weapon against Satan. The more scripture that is planted in our heart, the bigger and more dangerous is our Sword of the Spirit. Use your weapon, the Sword of the Spirit, by speaking the Word of God in faith.

With the power of the Holy Spirit, the Word of God, and our faith, we are to take back what the enemy has stolen from us. As believers, we need to reclaim our lives and establish the kingdom of God here on earth. We must march into the enemy's camp and take back what he has stolen from us. *"Yet when he is found, he must restore, sevenfold; he may have to give up all the substance of his house"* (Proverbs 6:31). There is a spiritual battle going on day and night. Being part of the Kingdom of Light, we will overcome by forcefully renouncing Satan's lies and agreeing with the truth. Our truth is the Word of God. Our Sword of the Spirit, the Word of God, needs to be sharpened and ready for action (Hebrews 4:12, Matthew 11:12).

OUR SPIRITUAL AUTHORITY: SPEAKING TO OUR MOUNTAIN

The LORD doesn't want us to stay baby Christians, but He wants us to grow up and mature spiritually. God tells us in the scriptures to speak to our mountain and not wait for someone else to move our mountain (Mark 11:22-23, Hebrews 5:12-14).

After Jesus died on the cross and resurrected from the dead, He gave His disciples spiritual authority on earth to do kingdom work in His name. Jesus paid the penalty on the cross for sin, curses, and sickness. We need to stand on Jesus's redemptive work on the cross and resist Satan, and he will flee. This means as His followers we agree with what Jesus has told us, and we must war against evil. If we are disobeying God, we are leaving the door open for Satan by our disobedience (2 Timothy 2:26).

According to Mark 11:22-23, we are to speak to our mountains. We are to speak to sickness, oppression, and our situations (our mountains). Examples of how to speak to our mountains: (1) "Sickness you must leave now, I command arthritis to leave my hands now in the name of Jesus Christ of Nazareth". (2) "As for me and my house, we serve the LORD, behind me Satan!" We need to believe in our heart the words we are saying or there is no effect (Mark 7:31-37).

We must speak in faith to our mountains and command sickness to leave. When you speak to your mountain, visualize your mountain moving and being thrown into the sea. If your mountain is for your knee to be healed, speak to your knee "knee you will walk with no pain, pain I command you to leave now in the name of Jesus Christ of Nazareth". I recently injured my ankle while walking and I sat down and commanded my ankle to be healed and restored. I laid my hands on my ankle and made a declaration that I would continue my walk with no pain and no injury. I waited about ten minutes and the pain was gone, and I continued on my walk. Praise the LORD! (Mark 11:22-23).

Sometimes "speaking to our mountain" will be speaking against Satan's lies. If Satan is trying to get you to agree with fear, rebuke and renounce fear out loud. Speak to it! "You must leave fear! I trust God and fear is a liar! Fear you must get out of here in the name of Jesus. Me and my house we serve the LORD, not fear".

God has given us the Keys of the Kingdom. We have the spiritual authority to speak on earth to our mountains and heaven will agree. When you give someone your house keys, you give them access to your home. When God gives us the "Keys to the Kingdom" we have the spiritual authority to do His work on earth and heaven agrees. Is sin, sickness, curses, or oppression ruling over you? We are to reign in life. We need to fight the good fight of faith regardless of how long the battle is. Put your faith in the only thing that is everlasting truth; Jesus Christ. Without Jesus Christ, there is no victory (Matthew 18:18, Matthew 16:19).

PERSONAL TESTIMONY: OUR SPIRITUAL AUTHORITY

Once I understood my spiritual authority, it was time to exercise it. I was a substitute teacher, and when I was substituting in a classroom, I had authority in that classroom. I used my authority in the classroom in conjunction with my spiritual authority as a child of God; and when the opportunity arose, I wanted to bless those people God put in my path. When there was difficulty in a classroom, I had my newfound truths to speak life in my classroom and help children handle situations that brought peace into the classroom. I worked in classrooms with disabled children and had opportunities to pray for them. One day I was a substitute teacher in a 4th grade classroom. This 4th grade boy looked very distressed. I went over and talked to him, and he was in despair. He was making eye contact with me, and his eyes were saying "help me". He stated his brother recently was discharged from the hospital after cutting himself. He told me his brother would laugh crazily and scarily, and that he was afraid of his 13-year-old brother. I knew this was demonic. A teacher at the school had told him to be positive, and he told me he was trying to be positive, but it wasn't working. This boy needed God's help, not the "be positive" outlook. As I talked to this boy, I found that he believed in Jesus. In the small amount of time I had with this boy, I gave him words to speak over the situation at home by using his spiritual authority as a believer. I told this little boy to pray to God and ask for His help. This boy agreed with me and said he would. Probably within ten minutes of talking to him, I noticed this boy seemed at peace. I know God knew the heart of this little boy and wanted to help him.

CHAPTER 15
Spiritual Warfare

Jesus won the battle over Satan and the kingdom of darkness. *"And having spoiled principalities and powers, He made a show of them openly, triumphing over them in it"* (Colossians 2:15). Now as His disciples we must stand at our post and enforce Jesus's victory. We are to appropriate the truth in our own life. What is spiritual warfare? Spiritual warfare is submitting to God and opposing/resisting Satan and his lies. *"Submit yourselves therefore to God. Resist the devil, and he will flee from you"* (James 4:7).

We need to be awakened to the fact that spiritual wars are going on day and night. If we choose to ignore this, we could fall into a trap. We are called to the truth, not to ignorance. Satan wants us to believe his lies and live a defeated life. But Christ wants us to live a victorious life by appropriating the truth in our lives. We need to be the enforcers of the victory Jesus won over Satan. We do this by agreeing with the Word of God and using the truth to come against the lies of Satan (Hosea 4:6, Colossians 2:14-15).

Our battle is not against fellow man but against the dark spiritual forces. When we stand against these dark spiritual forces, we are agreeing with God and saying no to our enemy (Satan and his kingdom). *"For we wrestle not against flesh and blood, but against principalities, against powers, against the rulers of the darkness of this world, against spiritual wickedness in high places"* (Ephesians 6:12). This verse says "we wrestle" against wickedness. Jesus was triumphant over Satan but now we must agree with that truth. In our spiritual warfare, we are coming from a place of victory, not of defeat. In the wrestling match with evil, Satan may have you pinned temporarily, but rise up with your spiritual authority and overcome. In a wrestling match, you must confront the enemy with truth. We are to fight our spiritual battles by prayer (using the Word of God) and fasting, using our spiritual authority, submitting to God by our obedience, being led by the Holy Spirit, and putting on the whole armor of God.

If we are ignorant of the spirit realm and spiritual battles, it does not stop Satan and his evil kingdom from attacking us. I know this because I used to be in ignorance, but it did not stop the enemy from tormenting me. When I learned how to fight my enemy in the spirit realm, my spiritual freedom began.

THE WHOLE ARMOR OF GOD

In Ephesians 6:10-18, we read about the whole armor of God. In verse 10, it states "...*be strong in the LORD, and in the power of His might*". When we are putting on the whole armor of God, His strength and power will be our protection. The whole armor of God is spiritual, not physical. According to verse 11, we are to "*stand against the wiles (schemes, trickery) of the devil.*" The word "stand" is defined in Greek as to make firm; to uphold or sustain the authority or force of anything; to stand immovable.

We wrestle with principalities, against powers, and against rulers of this dark world. The wrestling match between good and evil is very evident in our physical world, but the battle is spiritual. We can easily see with our physical eyes the troubles going on in the world, but with our spiritual eyes, we know the evil in the world is authorized by the powers of darkness in the spirit realm.

The Whole Armor of God:

(1) Belt of Truth (Stand having girded your loins with truth). We are to "stand" which is to establish and hold up the truth; God's truth. We need to know the Word of God so we recognize the lies of Satan (Ephesians 6:14).

(2) Put on the Breastplate of Righteousness. Romans 10:10 says, "*For with the heart man believes to righteousness, and with the mouth confession is made to salvation.*" When we put on the breastplate of righteousness, we stand knowing who we are in Christ, and we are sons of God and have been given authority to trample on all the lies of the enemy. The breastplate of righteousness protects our heart when we know we are the righteousness of God (Ephesians 6:14).

(3) Shod (bind) your feet with the Preparation of the Gospel of Peace. When we believe in the gospel (good news) of Jesus Christ, we should be prepared to share the good news. We are standing by, ready to meet

the challenge, to share the gospel. When we are abiding with the LORD, we are free from fear and at peace to do God's work on the earth (Ephesians 6:15).

(4) Take the <u>Shield of Faith</u>. Our shield of faith will extinguish the fiery darts (shots) of the evil one. Our faith is the power that brings heaven to earth. Satan loves when we walk in doubt and unbelief. Satan hates faith because he operates in fear (Ephesians 6:16).

(5) Take the <u>Helmet of Salvation</u>. When we take (receive, take up) the helmet of salvation, our salvation is our defense from Satan. The word "helmet" in Hebrew is the protection of the soul. When we believe in Jesus Christ as our LORD and Savior, we are brought from death to life (2 Samuel 22:3-4, Ephesians 6:17).

(6) Take the <u>Sword of the Spirit</u>. Our Sword of the Spirit is the Word of God. When Jesus was in the wilderness and Satan was tempting Him, Jesus spoke the Word of God to defeat the lies of Satan. The more scriptures we have planted in our hearts, the more dangerous our sword (Matthew 4:1-11, Ephesians 6:17).

(7) <u>Pray always with all prayer, in the Spirit</u>. When we pray, we are using the authority Jesus gave us to bring heaven to earth (Ephesians 6:18).

As soldiers for Jesus Christ, we can't go into battle without the Armor of God. When a solider gets deployed, he has preparations to make before he leaves for battle. His weapons are made ready. The same is true for a soldier of Jesus Christ. There are actions we do to prepare ourselves for battle. We need to know the weapons God has given us.

The Whole Armor of God is for the warrior! The LORD has given us this armor to fight the kingdom of darkness. Our battle is a faith battle (the good fight of faith). The battle is in the mind and heart. Our mind is not to conform to the patterns of this world and to bring into captivity every thought to the obedience of Christ. Our heart is to be kept pure and to stand in faith believing God's word (Romans 12:2, Proverbs 4:23).

The question isn't "will trouble come" but the question is "when trouble comes, am I prepared to come against the lies of Satan?" Don't wait until devastation comes into your life to seek God's truth on spiritual matters. Learn how to fight your spiritual battles before Satan shows up at your door. Don't let Satan steal, kill, or destroy you or your family. Satan is a trespasser. Post your no trespassing sign and stand on guard (Deuteronomy 30:19).

Don't compromise the truth because of the ways of this world. Live by the commands of your Heavenly Father. We are a new creation as believers. We are commanded to forgive, repent, and renounce lies. We are to stand in the spiritual authority God Almighty has given us as believers.

Below are some spiritual warfare prayers using the Word of God. When you pray using the Word of God, you are agreeing with God and enforcing His truth by your faith.

- Spiritual warfare prayer: The Word of God says that You (God) will cause my enemies that rise up against me to be defeated before my face. They will come out against me one way and flee before me seven ways. I thank you God for rescuing me from the hands of the enemy. Through Jesus's completed work on the cross, I am saved, healed, delivered, made whole, and preserved (Deuteronomy 28:7, 1 John 5:10-13).

- Spiritual warfare prayer: The LORD says in Isaiah 54:17 that no weapon formed against me will prosper and every tongue that rises up against me in judgment that I will condemn it. This is my heritage as a servant of the LORD and my righteousness is of the LORD. I come against those words spoken against me. I rebuke and condemn them in the name of Jesus Christ and as my heritage as a servant of the LORD.

- Spiritual warfare prayer: I renounce and rebuke the authority I gave fear because now I live in truth. Your word says in Hebrews 11:6 that without faith it is impossible to please You. And in 2 Timothy 1:7 Your Word says, *"For God has not given us the spirit of fear; but of power, and of love, and of a sound mind."* Father God, I thank you for giving me the power to overcome and live by faith.

CHAPTER 16

Spiritual Check-up

The journey for the Israelites from Egypt to Canaan was supposed to be an 11-day journey, but it took them 40 years. God wants to move us from bondage to freedom; from immature to mature believers. God was moving the Israelites from bondage in Egypt to freedom in Canaan. What took the Israelites such a long time to move out of captivity? The Israelites were disobedient to God; they were ungrateful, fearful, and idolatrous. What is keeping you from moving into your freedom or your next step with God? God wants us to be spiritually mature; He wants to move us forward into the plans He has for our life. There is kingdom work God has prepared in advance for us to do, but if we never move out of our bondage, we will never reach our full potential. When we have spiritually matured and gone from bondage to freedom, we can help others be set free!

Some believers may be stuck in bondage, others may be stuck in unbelief or fear, others may be unsure of what God's plans are for them, others may have found their freedom but don't know how to help others be set free. Wherever you are at, a spiritual check-up can help you locate where you are and make a course correction or help you to be intentional about your walk with the LORD.

It is wise to test ourselves to evaluate our spiritual condition. *"Test and evaluate yourselves to see whether you are in the faith and living your lives as [committed] believers. Examine yourselves [not me]! Or do you not recognize this about yourselves [by an ongoing experience] that Jesus Christ is in you, unless indeed you fail the test and are rejected as counterfeit?"* (2 Corinthians 13:5). We should examine whether we have opened the door to the enemy (Satan). We can only have one master, and we don't want sin to be our master. The more we know the Word of God, the more we will be able to discern good from evil. We are each responsible for our own sin and repentance.

We should periodically check the course of our spiritual life; are we staying on the narrow path? We should start each day in the Word of God and prayer. For our spiritual well-being and growth, it is a good safeguard to do a spiritual check-up.

We need to come before the LORD regularly and search our hearts and have heartfelt repentance for our sins. We should search our lives periodically to make sure we are not giving Satan any territory by our disobedience. It is important to examine ourselves and be sure that we are not holding "ought" towards someone that we thought we had forgiven (Leviticus 19:17-19, Mark 11:25).

Are we seeking the LORD for His plans for our lives? *"For we are His workmanship, created in Christ Jesus to good works, which God has before ordained that we should walk in them"* (Ephesians 2:10). He wants us to joyfully serve Him and seek Him for guidance to be led into the plans He has for us.

What is the plan for your life? Write down the vision the LORD has given you for your life. Then write down the steps to accomplish the vision. The LORD has a plan for our life and so does Satan. If we are intentional, we can have safeguards in place to assure we walk into the LORD's plan for our life. *"Then the LORD answered me and said, 'Write the vision and engrave it plainly on [clay] tablets so that the one who reads it will run. For the vision is yet for the appointed [future] time. It hurries toward the goal [of fulfillment]; it will not fail. Even though is delays, wait [patiently] for it, because it will certainly come; it will not delay"* (Habakkuk 2:2-3).

Part of our spiritual check-up should be to examine our spiritual beliefs. Are the truths we believe a truth from God or a lie from Satan? We need to go back and examine if what we believe is actually from the Word of God, a ritual, or a lie we have believed for a long time. Once the truth is revealed, the lie is exposed. We don't intentionally believe lies, but there can be a stronghold in our thinking that prevents us from seeing the truth. The lies I believed were exposed when I put aside what I thought was true and asked God to show me the truth. I had to go outside of my comfort zone and let the Holy Spirit guide me to the truth. We need to examine where our information comes from. Is our information coming from the Bible or did someone tell us something, and we assumed it was true? We need to study the Bible for ourselves to see if it is God's truth. It is unwise to live our lives by something someone told us without checking out the source ourselves. Make sure you align your beliefs with the Word of God. Also, use an accurate translation of the Bible and check the Greek and Hebrew translation of a word. I have found if you believe a specific word means something other than the true original meaning in the Bible, it can completely change what the verse in the Bible originally meant.

We should always be truth-seekers in our spiritual walk. God's word reveals we are in a time where many lies have seeped into our thinking; society believes many things that are deceptions. *"Now the Spirit speaks expressly, that in the latter times some shall depart from the faith, giving heed to seducing spirits, and doctrines of devils; speaking lies in hypocrisy; having their conscience seared with a hot iron; forbidding to marry, and commanding to abstain from meats, which God has created to be received with thanksgiving of them which believe and know the truth. For every creature of God is good, and nothing to be refused, if it be received with thanksgiving: For it is sanctified by the Word of God and prayer. If thou put the brethren in remembrance of these things, thou shalt be a good minister of Jesus Christ, nourished up in the words of faith and of good doctrine, whereunto thou has attained"* (1 Timothy 4:1-6). If God's word means what it says, God says we are to eat the food He has given us and pray before we eat and whatever we eat is sanctified. God wants us to be able to eat the food He has given us on the earth. This is just one example of how lies creep into our world and overtake God's truth.

The Word of God warns us of spiritual dangers we need to guard against. One of these very important warnings is the serious danger of pride. The LORD God wants us to humble ourselves because pride can bring us to destruction. According to 2 Corinthians 10:5, *"casting down imaginations, and every high (proud) thing that exalts itself against the knowledge of God . . ."* Pride can cause us to find faults in others while not seeing them in ourselves (Matthew 7:5). The LORD showed me that when I didn't want to receive help from others when I needed it, it was prideful. Pride comes in many different forms and can sneak in very quietly. On April 12, 2012, the New York Post wrote an article called "The Pride Before the Titanic's Fall" discussing the role pride played in the sinking of the Titanic. The Irish shipyard that built the Titanic said it was unsinkable. The article indicates "they did presume that competence and procedural mastery would guarantee unsinkability." The Word of God says in Proverbs 16:18 that pride goes before destruction. The Greek Strong's Concordance definition for pride is self-exaltation (self-absorption) which carries its own self-destructive vanity. In Hebrew, the definition of pride is exaltation (arrogance), lifting up. How can we examine our heart to determine if pride is present? Here are a few questions you can use to test for pride: 1) You easily find fault in others and not yourself. 2) You get defensive. 3) You get too concerned with how others perceive you. 4) The need for attention and praise. According to Proverbs 16:5, *"Everyone that is proud in heart is an abomination to the LORD. . ."* I am grateful the LORD showed me the error of my ways. With God's help, I can keep myself in check so I don't let pride abide in my heart.

We should be intentional in our spiritual walk. We are not running aimlessly in the good fight of faith. We should not be moving where the wind blows us, but as we make plans in our life, pray that God will direct our steps. Run your race without comparing yourself to others; therefore, you won't get off course. Don't define your worth by comparison because our identity is in Christ. *"Do you not know that in a race all the runners run (their very best to win), but only one receives the prize? Run [your race] in such a way that you may seize the prize and make it yours! Now every athlete who (goes into training and) competes in the games is disciplined and exercises self-control in all things. They do it to win a crown that withers, but we [do it to receive] an imperishable [crown that cannot wither]. Therefore I do not run without a definite goal; I do not flail around like one beating the air [just shadowing boxing]. But [like a boxer] I strictly discipline my body and make it my slave, so that, after I have preached [the gospel] to others, I myself will not somehow be disqualified [as unfit for service]"* (1 Corinthians 9:24-27).

We need to spiritually guard what we let our eyes see, what our ears hear, what our mind thinks, what our mouth speaks, and what we hold in our heart. Whatever is true, honest, just, pure, lovely, of good report, virtuous, praiseworthy, we are to keep our mind and heart on these things. As I have grown in my spiritual walk, God has refined me and removed worldly desires from my heart. I don't want to spend time doing things that are unfruitful for the kingdom of God. I value the time God has given me and want to complete the assignment He has given me to do.

Part of our spiritual check-up should include safeguards for our minds. In what ways can we check the condition of our minds? One way is to take an inventory of your mind; what do you spend your time thinking about? Actually, write a list of the top 5 things you spend your time thinking about. This will reveal a lot about the state of your mind. The state of your mind can affect your wellbeing. We can meditate on what we choose to meditate on with the power of the Holy Spirit and the Word of God. We will need to fight against wrong thinking, but it is worth warring against the lies of the enemy and wrong thinking. We will need to choose to disagree with evil and negative thinking. Jesus spoke to Satan using the Word of God when He was tempted, and we need to use the Word of God to fight against our wrong thoughts. *"And be not conformed to this world: but be transformed by the renewing of your mind, that you may prove what is that good, and acceptable, and perfect will of God"* (Romans 12:2).

In our spiritual walk, we want to be led by God in our decision-making process. Below are some statements that may help in this process. How to make good decisions:

1) Your decision should always line up with the Word of God.
2) Be patient, God does not rush us, but Satan does.
3) Bring your desires to a place of neutrality, you will then be able to hear from God.
4) Pray for wisdom. *"If any of you lacks wisdom, let him ask of God, who gives to all liberally and without reproach, and it will be given to him"* (James 1:5).
5) Pray for knowledge from the LORD to help you with your decision. *"Call on Me and I will answer you, and show you great and mighty things, which you know not"* (Jeremiah 33:3).
6) Be led by the Holy Spirit. The Holy Spirit will lead us, encourage us, comfort us, and guide us. But Satan's voice will rush us, push us, frighten us, confuse us, discourage us, obsess us, and condemn us.
7) We should have peace with our decision. *"Peace, I leave with you, My peace I give to you: not as the world gives, give I to you, Let not your hearts be troubled, neither let it be afraid"* (John 14:27).
8) We can seek wise counsel from believers we trust (Proverbs 12:15, Proverbs 11:14, Proverbs 15:22).
9) Trust and acknowledge the LORD in all your ways, according to Proverbs 3:5-6, and He will direct your steps.

Furthermore, regarding our spiritual check-up, we will look at the topic of "testing the spirits". We are spirit beings and part of our spiritual walk should include testing our spirit and the spirits of the people in our lives that influence us. We are spirit beings who live in a body with a soul. *"Beloved, believe not every spirit, but try the spirits whether they are of God: because many false prophets are gone out into the world. Hereby know you the Spirit of God: Every spirit that confesses that Jesus Christ is come in the flesh is of God: And every spirit that confesses not that Jesus Christ is come in the flesh is not of God: and this is that spirit of antichrist, whereof you have heard that it should come; and even now already is it in the world. You are of God, little children, and have overcome them: because greater is he that is in you, than he that is in the world. They are of the world, therefore speak they of the world, and the world hears them. We are of God: he that knows God hears us; he that is not of God hears not us. Hereby know we the spirit of truth, and the spirit of error"* (1 John 4:1-6). Therefore, we are to test the spirits to see if they are of God. Since all human beings are spirit beings, we are to test those spirits before they enter our lives, and we can also test ourselves to check our spiritual wellness and growth. How can we know if a spirit is not of God? What do the scriptures say about this? According to 1 John 4:1-6, we can separate the spirits into two categories: the spirit of truth or the spirit of error. Continuing with 1 John 4:1-6, we also learn that the first test is if the spirit confesses that Jesus Christ has come in the flesh is of God. Secondly, according to Matthew 7:15-20, we can test the Spirit by the fruit the spirit produces. If the spirit lives their life pursuing righteousness and their fruit is good fruit, the spirit is a spirit of truth. The words we speak, the actions we take, the things we listen to, the activities we do will all reveal something about our spiritual well-being. If we are following God's truth, there will be evidence in our life. How much evidence in your life is there to prove you are a disciple of Jesus Christ? Lastly, we can test the spirit by the evidence of love, joy, peace, long-suffering, gentleness, goodness, faith, meekness, and temperance (self-control) according to Galatians 5:22-23. As disciples of Jesus Christ, the Holy Spirit lives in us and guides us to follow Him and turn from evil.

Walk in the Spirit dear brothers and sisters. When we walk in the Spirit, we are listening to the Holy Spirit and are obedient. Following our own desires can get us into trouble. We should walk humbly before the LORD and listen to the Holy Spirit leading us and be obedient to His direction. *"This I say then, Walk in the Spirit, and ye shall not fulfill the lust of the flesh"* (Galatians 5:16).

As we grow in our spiritual walk, we become more and more like Christ. The more we abide in the LORD and seek His truth, God's truths are made known to us. A truth, we may think we understand, may be further revealed to us as God's mysteries are made known to us. Our spiritual growth and wellness will penetrate our body, mind, and soul. God desires our spiritual growth and maturity. He wants us to make it to the Promised Land and be set free! (1 Thessalonians 5:23)

CHAPTER 17

We Choose

God does not manipulate or control us, but He gives us the ability to choose. We are responsible for the choices we make in our life. What we sow into, we will reap. Our choices can reap good fruit or bad fruit in our lives. Our choices, whether good or bad, affect others. God has given us the freedom to choose; what will you do with your freedom? *"For you brethren, have been called to liberty; only do not use liberty for an opportunity for the flesh, but through love serve one another"* (Galatians 5:13).

Jesus said, in Matthew 28, all power has been given to Him in heaven and in the earth, and He continues to tell His disciples to teach all nations and baptize them. Furthermore, Jesus said that His disciples are to teach all His ways to the world. In Matthew 28:18-20 and Mark 16:15-20, Jesus gave His authority to His disciples to bring heaven to earth. After Jesus ascended into heaven, Jesus worked through His disciples confirming the Word with signs and wonders. Have you said yes to Jesus and to do His Kingdom work here on earth? His Kingdom's work includes preaching the gospel, healing the sick, setting the captive free, and however God leads us to bring heaven to earth through the power of the Holy Spirit. If you are a disciple of Jesus Christ, you choose to bring His Kingdom to earth!

We choose who we serve: *"And if it seems evil to you to serve the LORD, choose for yourselves this day whom you will serve, whether the gods which your fathers served that were on the other side of the River, or the gods of the Amorites, in whose land you dwell. But as for me and my house, we will serve the LORD"* (Joshua 24:15). Who will you serve? We choose whether we serve God or Satan. If we are serving the world, serving ourselves, or serving evil, we are not serving God. God says when we choose Him we must deny our selfish desires and live for Him. When we serve God, there will be giving of our time, treasure, and talent for God's Kingdom. God's ways are radically different than the ways of the world; there will be sacrifices for His Kingdom purposes. In Mark 8:34, Jesus said whoever follows Him will deny himself and take up his cross (self-denial, self-sacrifice) and follow Him.

We choose how we spend our time and spending time in prayer is vital to our spiritual life. When we choose to pray, we are agreeing with God's best for our life. By choosing to pray over our nation, pray over our family, pray over our futures, pray over our home, pray over our food, and pray a blessing over everything we bring into our home; we are choosing to agree with God that we want Him to bless everything in our lives and that Satan needs to keep his hands off of us.

We choose whose voice we listen to. Is the noise of the world so loud that we don't hear the LORD? *"Behold, I stand at the door, and knock: if any man hear my voice, and open the door, I will come in to him, and will sup with him, and he with me,"* (Revelation 3:20). Are we listening to the voice of an unbelieving friend, are we listening to the loud voice of worldly influences, are we listening to gossip? The choices we make every day with regard to what we listen to will affect whether we can hear our Heavenly Father's voice.

God was grieved when He saw the wickedness of man on the earth in Genesis 6:5. This scripture verse states that man's *"every imagination of the thoughts of his heart was only evil continually"*. We choose what we meditate on in our minds, and it is one of the most important choices that will reap either peace or turmoil in our life. When we have a thought, we have a choice to meditate on it or discard it. If we meditate on a thought long enough, it becomes part of our long term memory and can affect future thoughts and actions. We need to be mindful of our thoughts and choose to discard wrong and sinful thinking. *"For to be carnally minded is death; but to be spiritually minded is life and peace"* (Romans 8:6).

Our choices include guarding our mind and heart. When we choose to protect our mind and heart, we will be purposefully making choices to lead our life down the right path. The gateways to the soul are our mind and heart. God and Satan are both battling for our mind and heart. What we spend time meditating on is our choice. What we allow into our heart is our choice (Proverbs 4:23, Philippians 4:7-8).

We choose to stand firm in faith, or not. Are we walking in doubt, unbelief, fear, or faith? According to 1 Peter 1:7, *"That the genuineness of your faith, being much more precious than gold that perishes, though it is tested by fire, may be found to praise, honor, and glory at the revelation of Jesus Christ."* As believers, we need to be committed to fighting the good fight of faith. We will need to speak words of faith when others are growing weak; we will need to act in faith when circumstances in the physical look dim; and we will need to continue praying in faith and persevere.

We are told, in the Word of God, to speak to our mountain. When there is a mountain to move, there is work to be done. It is a choice to fight the good fight of faith and use your spiritual authority and speak to your mountain. According to Mark 11:23 says, *"For verily I say to you, that whosoever shall say unto this mountain, Be thou removed, and be thou cast into the sea; and shall not doubt in his heart, but shall believe that those things which he saith shall come to pass; he shall have whatsoever he saith."* What is your mountain that you need to be moved? Make a decision that your mountain needs to be moved and move to the frontline of your battle.

We choose our words. We choose either gossip or speaking in love. We choose either to complain or to praise. We choose to speak blessings or curses. We choose life or death with the words of our mouth. *"Death and life are in the power of the tongue: and they that love it shall eat (consume) the fruit (produce) thereof"* (Proverbs 18:21). Do we understand the power of our words and actions, and that we are releasing life or death, good or evil, blessing or curses with our words and actions? *"See I have set before you today life and good, death and evil, in that I command you today to love the LORD your God, to walk in His ways, and to keep His commandments, His statutes, and His judgments, that you may live and multiply; and the LORD your God will bless you in the land which you go to possess. But if your heart turns away, so that you do not hear, and are drawn away, and worship other gods and serve them, I announce to you that you shall surely perish; you shall not prolong your days in the land which you cross over the Jordan to go in and possess. I call heaven and earth as witnesses today against you, that I have set before you life and death, blessing and cursing: therefore choose life, that both you and your descendants may live; that you may love the LORD your God, that you obey His voice, and that you may cling to Him, for He is your life and the length of your days and that you may dwell in the land which the LORD swore to your fathers, to Abraham, Isaac, and Jacob, to give them"* (Deuteronomy 30:15-20).

The choices we make will lead us in the direction we are going. If we agree with the world, we are headed in a wide path of deception. If we agree with the lies of Satan, we are headed into the snares of Satan's plans for our life. But if we agree with God and obey Him, we are headed on the path to abundant life which will free our body, mind, and soul.

TRIALS AND TEMPTATIONS

During a trial or temptation, what we agree with and the choices we make will determine if we glorify God or not. <u>Choose wisely</u>!

> 1) According to 2 Timothy 3:12, *"Yea, and all that will live godly in Christ Jesus shall suffer persecution."* If we are living godly lives, we will not be making friends with the world. <u>Choose wisely</u>!
> 2) According to 1 Peter 4:12-13, *"Beloved, do not think it strange concerning the fiery trial which is to try you, as though some strange thing happened to you; but rejoice to the extent that you partake of Christ's sufferings, that when His glory is revealed, you may also be glad with exceeding joy."* These scripture verses reminds us to not focus on our difficult circumstances but to continue to praise God, and His glory will be shown. <u>Choose wisely</u>!
> 3) What does the Bible say about temptation, being tested, and leaving an open door for the enemy? Satan harasses mankind by tempting them to do evil and to destroy the work of God. In regards to being tested, metal is tested for its purity. God tests people to show their heart and thoughts. The way we handle the test or trial will either glorify God or open the door to the enemy. What opens the door to the enemy? If we have disobeyed God, we are opening the door to Satan and agreeing with him. If we listen to Satan's lies and don't cast them down, we are submitting to him and his evil plans for our life. <u>Choose wisely</u>! (Ephesians 4:26-27, 1 Peter 1:7)
> 4) According to Exodus 20:20, *"And Moses said to the people, 'Do not fear; for God has come to test you, and that His fear may be before you, so that you may not sin.'"* When we follow God in obedience, He sanctifies us, and He leads us to our eternal home. <u>Choose wisely</u>! (2 Corinthians 3:18)

PERSONAL TESTIMONY OF MY FREE WILL

There was a time in my life where I was dismayed and didn't know how to make changes in my life. I felt like a prisoner with my hands tied. I felt like I couldn't change things in my own life. I was unhappy but didn't have a clue what to do. God used a Christian radio talk show that was called "Intentional Living" with Dr. Randy Carlson. His wisdom to his listeners gave me hope and direction. Sometimes you just get stuck in the mud, and you need someone to push you out. I felt God used Dr. Carlson's radio show to show me I wasn't powerless. God has given me a spirit of power, love, and sound mind. I could make changes in my life because I was a child of God, and God is my Defender, Protector, Friend, Strength, Courage, and Guide. I had a choice; I had lots of choices, and I was going to start to change and live my life more abundantly!!

PERSONAL TESTIMONY – THE CHOICE TO SERVE GOD

Clay and his wife were on the prayer team at my church, and they were praying for our family. Clay would send me encouraging scripture and shared with me his website with spiritual poems. We would discuss spiritual truths over email. Clay and his wife faithfully prayed for our family for about a year and a half. His communication with me was very important to me and gave me hope. Later I found out Clay passed away, and I was never able to meet him. One of the last communications we had was when I told him I felt led to write a book on spiritual truths, and what I have learned from being refined in the fire. Clay's email response was, "do it with all your heart!" Clay and his wife helped bring me hope during a difficult time. I was never able to meet him or thank him, but I will never forget him. Clay chose to serve God to the end of his life on earth. Clay's choice to serve God blessed my life, and I am sure many others.

CHAPTER 18

God's Hospital: Healing, Deliverance, and Wholeness

As I mentioned earlier, I had a vision at a very dark time in my life. I saw this white sterile-looking laboratory where there were ledges all around the various levels of the building. The kingdom of darkness would pull one family member, out at a time, on a ledge and try experiments on them. These experiments were deceptions and lies. Satan was preying on us to see what lies or traps each family member would fall into. As I now have knowledge of the deceptions of Satan, I keep my shield of faith up and stand in truth to receive God's freedom and healing through Jesus Christ. As God kept revealing His truth to me, I grew in knowledge of His freedom. I had a second vision of steps leading to physical healing, deliverance, and freedom from all bondage. This vision of God's hospital had floors in it like a hospital would have floors for different levels of trauma and different treatment. These floors or steps led to God's Hospital where people were set free. God has an order in His creation and when things are out of His divine order, things go wrong. He wants His children set free and discharged from the hospital!

A.) HEALING – GOD'S HOSPITAL

In Luke 8:43-44, the woman having an issue of blood for twelve years had spent all of her living on physicians and was not healed. She touched the garment of Jesus and was immediately healed. A touch from Jesus changes our lives.

God wants us healed of all diseases according to Psalm 103:2-3. God's name *Jehovah-Rapha* means the God Who Heals. God does not want us sick. Satan wants us sick. John 10:10 says, *"The thief does not come except to steal, and to kill, and to destroy. I have come that they may have life, and that they may have it more abundantly"* (Exodus 15:26).

Jesus bore our sin and sickness on the cross. We are redeemed from the curse of sin and sickness. Jesus cleared the debt we owed. Matthew 8:17 says, *"He Himself took our infirmities and bore our sicknesses."* We are victorious through the victory Jesus won on the cross. According to Mark 16:15-18, the disciples of Jesus Christ are to lay hands on the sick, and they will recover. God wants His disciples to bring His Kingdom to earth by using our spiritual authority to lay hands on the sick.

God wants us healthy and healed. God's will for our life is that we never get sick, but if we do, His desire is that we are well. *"And Jesus went about all the cities and villages, teaching in their synagogues, and preaching the gospel of the kingdom, and healing every sickness and every disease among the people"* (Matthew 9:35).

Jesus is the Light of the world. When we follow the Light, the blood of Jesus cleanses us from all sin. Light gives health. Darkness brings sickness. *"The eye is the lamp of your body. When your eye is clear (spiritually perceptive, focused on God), your whole body also is full of light (benefiting from God's precepts). But when it is bad (spiritually blind), your body also is full of darkness (devoid of God's word)"* (Luke 11:34).

God's medicine is the Word of God. The Word of God is so amazingly powerful that it can penetrate to dividing soul and spirit. Once the Word of God is in our heart, it pumps through the entire body and has healing power. *"For the Word of God is living and powerful, and sharper than any two-edged sword, piercing even to the division of soul and spirit, and of joints and marrow, and is a discerner of the thoughts and intents of the heart"* (Hebrews 4:12).

We are told in Matthew 10:8, *"Heal the sick, cleanse the lepers, raise the dead, cast out demons. Freely you have received, freely give."* Jesus's healing power is for the physical body, the mind, and the soul. There are various scriptures detailing how a wounded soul can hurt the physical body. According to Proverbs 3:7-8, *"Be not wise in thine own eyes: fear the LORD, and depart from evil. It shall be health to thy navel, and marrow to thy bones."* According to Psalm 147:3, *"He healeth the broken in heart, and bindeth up their wounds."* Jesus's healing power restores the body, mind, and soul. Additionally recorded in Luke 6:18, *"And they that were vexed with unclean spirits: and they were healed."* Through the power of Jesus, unclean spirits are cast out and sickness flees.

When we lay hands on the sick for healing, we have the spiritual authority to speak to the sickness. Jesus is our example and Jesus spoke to the sickness while laying hands on the sick. God has given us the spiritual authority to heal the sick.

God Almighty is our Great Physician. He is Jehovah-Rapha, the God Who Heals. *". . . Who heals all your diseases"* (Psalm 103:3). Are we suffering from things that are not His will? God wants us healed so shouldn't we seek our healing through our Healer, believing He wants us healed instead of believing that He wants us to suffer in sickness. *"Therefore let those who suffer according to the will of God commit their souls to Him in doing good, as to a faithful Creator"* (1 Peter 4:19). **Shouldn't we suffer for the truth, not a lie of the enemy?** I do not believe God wants us sick; I believe God is the Healer and wants us completely healed. Satan wants us sick and wants us to stay sick so we can't fulfill the plans God has for our life.

According to John Hopkins Medicine, an article called <u>Forgiveness: Your Health Depends On It</u> states that being hurt and disappointed has an enormous impact on our body. It states chronic anger puts us into a fight or flight mode and results in changes in heart rate, blood pressure, and the immune response. Additionally, Dr. Steven Standiford, Chief of Surgery from Cancer Treatment Centers of America, states that refusing to forgive others makes people sick and keeps them sick. From this same article, Dr. Michael Barry, a pastor, and author of the book <u>The Forgiveness Project</u> states that 61 percent of cancer patients have problems with forgiving others. He indicates half of them have severe forgiveness issues.

There can be physical illnesses that are connected to soul wounds or spiritual root issues. Both aspects can be examined to help you identify the issue and how to address it. Below are some questions to identify possible problems. For further examination of spiritual root issues see my chapter on <u>Spiritual Roots</u>.

We may want to test our soul to see if there is a wound that was never dealt with and is causing us harm. God wants us healed and healthy. We can test ourselves and see if there is a correlation to a physical illness and a soul wound. We need to release harmful things that are in our soul; it could be a person we thought we forgave but we still are holding bitterness towards them, or it could be regret and we need to forgive ourselves. *"Beloved, I wish above all things that you may prosper and be in health, even as your soul prospers"* (3 John 1:2).

Below are some questions that may help you determine if there is a possible correlation between a physical sickness and a soul wound. (Determining this will either lead you to seek healing for the soul first and then the body will follow, or it is a physical healing of the body only that is needed.)

1) Most importantly, is the Holy Spirit bringing anything to your attention that you need to deal with or repent of?
2) Are you harboring unforgiveness towards someone, towards yourself, or towards God?
3) Are you engaging in repetitive sin that you refuse to remove from your life?
4) Do you love God, yourself, and others?
5) Does fear reside in your life?
6) Test your thoughts and heart with the Word of God. Are any of your thoughts contrary to the Word of God? Do you have wrong thinking patterns? Ask someone you trust to help you examine this.
7) Is your soul wounded? Are you holding on to past pain, regret, etc.?
8) Do you have shame or guilt that you haven't released?

These are just a few questions you can use to test your soul health. Pray and ask God to reveal to you if there is any darkness in you that He needs to shine the light on. Additionally, if you have someone you trust, they can help you walk through the above questions and help shed some light on the possible dark places you may have hidden deep in your soul.

Recorded in Proverbs 3:1-8; *"My son, do not forget my law; but let your heart keep my commandments; for length of days, and long life, and peace they will add to you. Let not mercy and truth forsake you; bind them around your neck; write them on the tablet of your heart, and so find favor and high esteem in the sight of God and man. Trust in the LORD with all your heart, and lean not on your own understanding; in all your ways acknowledge Him, and He shall direct your path. Do not be wise in your own eyes; fear the LORD and depart from evil. It will be health to your flesh, and strength to your bones."*

We are soldiers of Jesus Christ fighting the good fight of faith which includes faith for healing and deliverance. Abraham died in faith not having received the promise. He did not see the Promised Land while he was alive, but he still had faith until death. Soldiers of faith will believe until death in the promises of Jesus Christ. We are fighting the good fight of faith; and while in the battle, we have faith in God's word and promises. Our faith until death will reap good fruit to us and our seed; like Abraham's faithfulness reaped fruit to his seed. We can transform our bloodlines with faith like Abraham. Faith is the substance of things hoped for and the evidence of things not seen. *"Therefore it is of faith, that it might be by grace; to the end the promise might* be sure to all the seed; not to that only which is of the law, but to that also which is of the faith of Abraham; who is the father of us all. (As it is written, I have made you a father of many nations,) before Him whom he believed, even God, who makes alive the dead, and calls those things which he not as though they were. Who against hope believed in hope, that he might become the father of many nations; according to that which was spoken, So shall your seed be" (Romans 4:16-18).*

PERSONAL TESTIMONY

I not only believe in Jesus Christ as my LORD and Savior, but He is my Healer too. I had nerve damage as a result of a preventative medical procedure. The medical worker was quite aggressive when performing the procedure, and I was left with nerve damage that was quite painful. My sister, Paula, had me lay down on the couch, and she laid hands on me. Paula called it "spiritual surgery". She used her authority as a believer in Jesus Christ and spoke health and healing over my body. God completely healed me. I praise God for all He has done for me!!

B.) DELIVERANCE - GOD'S HOSPITAL

What is deliverance? Deliverance is to deliver someone out of the hands of Satan and his kingdom of darkness. *"You are my hiding place; You shall preserve me from trouble; You shall surround me with songs of deliverance"* (Psalm 32:7). Jesus overcame sin and Satan when he paid the price for our sins on the cross and rose again. Jesus was tempted in the wilderness by Satan, and Jesus overcame Satan with the Word of God. We will likewise be tempted by Satan and need to overcome. If Satan gains any ground in our lives and we are oppressed by him and his lies, we will need to get delivered out of his evil hands. According to Luke 10:17-19, *"And the seventy returned again with joy, saying, LORD, even the devils are subject to us through Your name. And He said to them, I beheld Satan as lightning fall from heaven. Behold, I give to you power to tread on serpents and scorpions, and over all the power of the enemy: and nothing shall by any means hurt you."*

We need to be overcomers. *"To him that overcomes will I grant to sit with me in My throne, even as I also overcame, and am set down with my Father in His throne"* (Revelation 3:21). To overcome is to prevail; to win the case; to overcome the adversary's devices. Since God said we are overcomers, there is something to overcome. We must overcome by agreeing with the truth of God and disagreeing with the lies of Satan; we do this by our obedience to the LORD. We are to submit to God. Submitting to God is humbling ourselves and yielding to God's direction. If we submit to the world, or our own way of thinking, or the lies of Satan; we are in opposition to God. *"And they overcame him by the blood of the Lamb, and by the word of their testimony; and they loved not their lives unto the death"* (Revelation 12:11).

A) TEST YOURSELF. We need to look at our lives and test whether Satan has gained any ground in our lives. If so, we need to kick him out! Below are some questions to test this. You can have someone you trust help you expose any areas of darkness in your life. By bringing the darkness into the light, you are able to recognize the lie in your mind or soul; and therefore, not allow the darkness further access to you. Additionally, bringing the darkness into the light will expose and destroy the lies of Satan, and then the evil can be cast out (Mark 4:22).

1) <u>Are you willfully sinning</u>? *"For if we sin willfully after that we have received the knowledge of the truth, there remaineth no more sacrifice for sins, but a certain fearful looking for of judgment and fiery indignation, which shall devour the adversaries"* (Hebrews 10:26-27). God says the believer should not be practicing to sin.

2) Pray and ask God to <u>reveal any lies you are believing</u>. Satan is the father of lies and tries to deceive us. We need to renounce and rebuke any lies we agreed with and repent of this. The LORD says it is our choice to choose life or death, blessings or curses. We need to look at our lives and test whether we have agreed with Satan and have been deceived. We have dominion here on earth over evil. We are God's children, and He has given us dominion over evil; stand firm and come out of agreement with any deceptions Satan has taught you (Psalm 115:16, Luke 10:19, 1 John 4:4).

3) <u>Is your soul anchored in anything other than God</u>? If we are tied to someone's soul and we let them influence us, they can pull us away from the LORD. The LORD is to be our first love, and He won't take second place! *"If thy brother, the son of thy mother, or thy son, or thy daughter, or the wife of thy bosom, or thy friend, which is as thine own soul, entice thee secretly, saying, Let us go and serve other gods, which thou hast not known, thou, nor thy fathers"* (Deuteronomy 13:6).

4) <u>Are you putting someone or something above God in your life</u>? In today's world, idolatry may look different from Bible times, but it is equally, if not more, destructive and in opposition to God. In today's world, people idolize their bodies, beauty, intelligence, money, their homes, their pets, their children, their status, their political viewpoint, their own opinion, certain relationships, music, technology, working out, their image, etc. What you worship is what you idolize. What is your devotion to? What

do you adore? Make a list of the top five things you spend your time and money on. Where is God on the list?

5) *"Now the Spirit speaketh expressly, that in the <u>latter times some shall depart from the faith, giving heed to seducing spirits, and doctrines of devils; Speaking lies in hypocrisy; having their conscience seared with a hot iron . . .</u>"* (1 Timothy 4:1-16). Ask the LORD in prayer if you are grounded in truth. Allow the Holy Spirit to lead you into more truth. Don't allow fear to block your growth. We can all be deceived if we don't allow the Holy Spirit to lead us.

6) <u>Are you oppressed with an evil spirit?</u> *"And they that were vexed with unclean spirits: and they were healed"* (Luke 6:18). Later in this chapter, I go into detail regarding demons and oppression.

7) A stronghold is a fortress or fortified place. In our lives, we can have a good stronghold when God is our fortress but when something sets itself up against God, we can have an evil stronghold in our life. *"For though we walk in the flesh, we do not war according to the flesh. For the weapons of our warfare are not carnal but mighty in God for pulling down strongholds, casting down arguments and every high thing that exalts itself against the knowledge of God, bringing every thought into captivity to the obedience of Christ"* (2 Corinthians 10:3-5). <u>Do you have any strongholds in your life?</u> Strongholds could be anger, anxiety, lying, laziness, pride, bitterness, depression, unforgiveness, addictions, sexual sins, manipulation, rebellion, rejection, unloving towards self or others, and more.

8) <u>Are you cursing yourself or others with your words?</u> *"Out of the same mouth proceedeth blessing and cursing. My brethren, these things ought not so to be"* (James 3:10). The LORD tells us we speak life or death with our mouth. We need to test everything we say. We are accountable for our idle words. If there has been a word curse spoken over you by your own words or someone else's words, repent of these words. Then break the word curse spoken, in the name of Jesus Christ, according to Galatians 3:13-15. We also have the authority according to Isaiah 54:17 to condemn every tongue that rises up against us in judgment.

9) <u>If our soul is wounded, we need healing</u>. A soul wound can distort our thinking and decision-making process. Someone with a soul wound will be more likely to listen to fleshly desires than

the Holy Spirit. Our soul can be wounded from sin, disobedience, a past hurt, etc. These wounds can be deep inside our soul, and we may not realize the wound is there. We can ask God to reveal to us any soul wounds we need to deal with. We can deal with our soul wound by recognizing our true feelings at the time it occurred; speaking the truth from that experience; repent or forgive depending which applies; and pray that through the power of Jesus's completed work on the cross, you are healed. Jesus Christ paid the debt for our iniquities and with His stripes, we are healed. The power of the Holy Spirit will heal the soul. By recognizing the past wound, we are now aware of how taking an offense is not God's will for our life. Therefore, we choose who we serve, God or Satan. We may not even be aware we are making a choice between good or evil, God or Satan. In Joshua 24:15, God's word says we do choose who we serve. When we serve God, we are agreeing with His plans for our life and doing things His way.

DELIVERANCE AND EVIL SPIRITS (DEMONS)

Believers in Jesus Christ can't be possessed by demons because the Holy Spirit dwells in the believer. But believers can be oppressed, influenced, or infected with demons. Demons need to be cast out (removed from our lives). During Jesus's ministry on earth, He healed many with sicknesses and many of these occasions, He also cast out demons. He commissioned His disciples to continue this work (Mark 16:15-18).

How do we get delivered if we are tormented by evil spirits, or how do we help someone get delivered from evil spirits? James 4:7-10 gives us the process of how to get Satan to flee from us. *"Therefore submit to God. Resist the devil and he will flee from you. Draw near to God and He will draw near to you. Cleanse your hands, you sinners, and purify your hearts, you double-minded. Lament and mourn and weep! Let your laughter be turned to mourning and your joy to gloom. Humble yourselves in the sight of the LORD, and He will lift you up."* The Word of God says to submit to God, resist the devil, and the devil will flee. First of all, what does submitting to God look like? Obeying God is submitting to Him. If we don't know the Word of God, our lack of knowledge will hinder our obedience. Secondly, we are to resist the devil which is to oppose him. We need to stand against Satan by coming against him with the Word of God. We need to know the clear difference between good and evil, truth and deception, and we will then recognize Satan's schemes. When we have the Word of God planted in our heart and we are obedient to God, we will be able to speak the scriptures in faith and Satan will flee (Galatians 5:1).

What are our weapons of warfare to fight Satan and his evil kingdom? 2 Corinthians 10:4-5, *"For the weapons of our warfare are not carnal but mighty in God for pulling down strongholds, casting down arguments and every high thing that exalts itself against the knowledge of God, bringing every thought into captivity to the obedience of Christ, and being ready to punish all disobedience when your obedience is fulfilled."* There is a spiritual battle to control our mind and draw us away from God and His truth, but the Holy Spirit will speak life to us and reveal the truth. We need our minds to be renewed according to Romans 12:2. God would not have told us to cast down arguments and to bring every thought into captivity to the obedience of Christ if it was not possible for us to do so (2 Corinthians 10:3-5).

Jesus having spoiled principalities and powers made a show of them openly, triumphing over them according to Colossians 2:15. Therefore, we also will overcome Satan as we humble ourselves before God. *"Humble yourself in the sight of the LORD, and He shall lift you up"* (James 4:10).

We are not to tolerate evil but confront evil. In Revelation 2:20, Jesus spoke to a church and told them they were allowing evil, and it was harming them. Learning how to confront evil and sin needs to be practiced; thereby, we will recognize evil and then be able to confront it. We will need to confront evil, in the spirit realm, with prayer and in the physical realm by declaring truth when a lie is spoken. In Revelation 12:11, the Word of God says we will overcome Satan by the blood of the Lamb and by our testimony (witness). Jesus has won the victory over Satan, but we will now enforce this victory in our own lives.

Deliverance is a confrontation with evil. There is no specific step-by-step process for deliverance, but seek God's word for His truth. Study the Word of God and notice how Jesus set the captives free by casting out demons. Once you have been delivered, abiding in the LORD is essential to remain free. As you continue humbling yourself before God and hating Satan, sin, and evil; the Holy Spirit will guide you into all truth and into the steps for your continued freedom. When we know the truth (Word of God) and we have faith, we will then be able to walk in truth, serve truth, and confront the enemy with truth (See Luke 11:24-26).

Everything we do as believers has to be done in faith. When we seek healing and deliverance, we need to stand in faith and proclaim the Word of God; thereby, we are proclaiming our spiritual authority over the darkness. The darkness then loses its power. An example of a prayer would be: LORD Almighty, I renounce and rebuke any evil spirit that gained access in my life and I receive your promise of healing and deliverance in the name of Jesus Christ of Nazareth. Furthermore, according to Luke 10:19, You have given me authority over all the power of the enemy and nothing shall by any means hurt me. Satan, I cast you out of my life! I thank and praise you God for my victory through Jesus Christ.

EVIL SPIRITS (DEMONS): Demons (evil spirits) are part of Satan's evil kingdom. Demons torment human beings and try to get people to agree with their evil plans. When we agree with their evil, they are able to conduct their destructive business here on earth with our cooperation. We may not realize this is happening and that is why having knowledge of Satan and his devices make us able to detect and sound the alarm to their evil. People are not our enemies, but Satan wants us to think they are. Below are some scripture verses where demonic spirits are spoken of in scripture.

> Mark 9:17, Mark 9:25, Matthew 9:32-33 – deaf and dumb spirit
> Acts 16:16 – the spirit of divination (fortune-telling)
> 1 Timothy 4:1 – seducing spirit
> 2 Timothy 1:7- the spirit of fear
> 1 John 4:6 – the spirit of error (falsehood)
> Numbers 5:14, Numbers 5:30 – the spirit of jealousy
> Judges 9:23, 1 Samuel 16:14-23, 1 Samuel 18:10, 1 Samuel 19:9 – evil spirits
> 1 Kings 22:22, 2 Chronicles 18:20-22– lying spirits
> Isaiah 29:10 – the spirit of deep sleep
> Isaiah 61:3 – the spirit of heaviness
> Hosea 4:12, Hosea 5:4 – the spirit of whoredoms
> Zechariah 13:2 – unclean spirits
> Luke 8:2 – Mary Magdalene had 7 demons cast out of her

If someone is oppressed with demonic influence, there will be signs of torment. The following scriptures detail oppression and the demonic influence (Luke 4:35, Acts 10:38, 1 Timothy 4:1-3, 1 Kings 22:22, 1 Kings 18:26-28, Mark 9:17, Mark 1:26, Mark 7:30, Matthew 9:32-33, Matthew 12:22, Matthew 17:15, Matthew 4:24, Acts 19:16, Acts 16:16, 1 Samuel 16:14-16, 1 Samuel 18:9-11, Luke 11:14, Luke 8:27, Luke 8:35-36, Luke 13:16, Luke 9:42, John 10:10, John 8:44, John 13:27).

Demons entice, harass, torture, compel, enslave, cause addiction, defile, deceive, and attack the physical body, mind, and soul. In the Bible, Jesus cast out demons. Fight to be set free and have the deliverance God wants for you. Humility is essential; pride will prevent your deliverance or healing. The spiritual fight to be set free is not a physical fight but a fight using God's word and your faith to stand in truth. The lies of Satan will be exposed when you align your thinking and heart with the Word of God. The Word of God will expose the enemy's lies. Pray and listen to the Holy Spirit; He is your Guide and will lead you into your freedom (Matthew 8:28-34).

When someone is seeking to be delivered from the demonic, the demons need to be exposed, weakened, and cast out. As the person comes back under God's order, the evil spirits will loosen their hold on the person. We must hate sin, Satan and his evil kingdom. Satan, the Accuser, is speaking against us day and night. He is looking for someone to accuse. The Word of God is our legal document to stand on. The truth in the Word of God sets us free. Seek the truth in the Word of God and meditate on it until it is planted in your heart (Revelation 12:10-11).

When Jesus walked the earth, He cast out demons (Mark 1:23-28). A large part of Jesus Christ's ministry on earth was casting out demons. In Mark 16:17 after Jesus's resurrection, He said to His disciples, *"And these signs shall follow them that believe; in My name shall they cast out devils . . ."* I have been to two different deliverance ministries seeking the truth. I have listened to over 80 hours plus of deliverance training and teaching from about four different deliverance ministries in search of more truth. Deliverance needs to begin with hearing and receiving truth from the Word of God to dispel the lies of Satan. I have witnessed amazing deliverances. I was delivered from a neck problem I had for about 15 years. The ministry leader commanded the yoke I was carrying to leave. After deliverance, I could turn my head all the way to the right which I hadn't been able to do for many years. The pressure on my neck was gone. After I left the deliverance conference, on my drive home, I continued to receive more healing in my neck. God wants us free of all bondage. Many people aren't even aware they are in bondage; they have been deceived by Satan. I didn't even know my neck problem was bondage until freedom came. Praise the LORD for His goodness even in the midst of my ignorance.

PERSONAL TESTIMONY

I made a decision to get baptized again when I was led to renounce fear in my life. On my baptism day, I renounced fear and read 2 Timothy 1:7, *"For God hath not given us the spirit of fear; but of power, and of love, and of a sound mind."* They went to baptize me and afterwards they said, "we have never had this happen before, but she did not fully get immersed so we want to baptize her the correct way and immerse her completely." Satan was trying to steal my deliverance that day. The spirit of fear was fighting to stay in my life, but praise the LORD, it had to leave!! I am very grateful the pastor made sure I was baptized correctly because I wanted freedom from fear. Ephesians 6:12 says <u>we wrestle</u> with the evil kingdom and that day it was a wrestling match and I won!

C.) OUR WHOLENESS – GOD'S HOSPITAL

God's Hospital provides physical and spiritual wholeness. The spiritual IV (intravenous) therapy that God's Hospital offers is the love of the Father, the power of the Holy Spirit, and a sound mind from the Word of God through Jesus Christ. The spiritual IV's (intravenous) central supply line is the "Great I AM" who supplies all our needs. We receive God's spiritual IV (intravenous) therapy by faith. He is the living well that never dries up and gives us all we need. God's spiritual IV (intravenous) supplies all the needs of His people through the Father, Son, Holy Spirit, and the Word of God. He is our "I AM" and fulfills all our needs (2 Timothy 1:7, Exodus 3:14).

God wants our body, soul, and spirit preserved blameless. If there is a problem in one area of our being, it can affect the whole. When we seek the LORD regularly for guidance, He will help us make a course correction when necessary. His guidance and our obedience will keep us on the narrow path. *"And the very God of peace sanctify you wholly; and I pray God your whole spirit and soul and body be preserved blameless to the coming of our LORD Jesus Christ"* (1 Thessalonians 5:23-24).

A) Body: We were bought with a price, and we are to glorify God with our bodies (1 Corinthians 6:20).

B) Inner man: Our inner being consists of our spirit, soul, mind, and conscience. *"Behold, You desire truth in the inward parts: and in the hidden part You shall make me to know wisdom"* (Psalm 51:6).

1) *Our Spirit*: After we have accepted Jesus as our personal LORD and Savior, the Holy Spirit dwells in us. First Corinthians 3:16, *"Do you not know that you are the temple of God and that the Spirit of God dwells in you?"* The Holy Spirit speaks to our spirit. The Holy Spirit is the Spirit of truth and will guide us into all truth.

2) *Soul*: Our soul is our emotions and will. The soul receives truth from our spirit, and by our free will, we will either listen to our spirit or listen to the flesh. Additionally in Romans 8:13, the sinful deeds of the flesh (body) will try to get our soul to agree, but we need to listen to the Holy Spirit and put to death the sinful deeds of the flesh. God created us with free will to say no to the lust of the flesh. Our soul is sensitive and can get wounded. *"He heals the broken in heart, and binds up their wounds"* (Psalm 147:3). The wounded soul is more likely to listen to fleshly desires. It is important to evaluate the condition of our soul. If our soul is wounded, it is important to diagnose the soul issue. We need to be truthful about our hurts, pain, sin, or disobedience. Recognizing and identifying the wound is the first step. Secondly, we need to either repent or forgive whichever applies to our situation. Finally, pray that your wound is healed through the completed work of Jesus Christ on the cross. The healing power of the Holy Spirit will heal our wounds.

3) <u>Mind</u>: Our minds are an absolutely amazing creation by God. With our imaginations, amazing things are created. With the powerful ability of our minds, we must be mindful of what we let into our thoughts. We need to be mindful of what we are letting our imaginations create. Are we agreeing with God in our thoughts and imaginations or are we agreeing with Satan? God knows our thoughts and intents. Is He pleased with our thoughts? According to 2 Corinthians 10:5, *"Casting down imaginations, and every high thing that exalts itself against the knowledge of God, and bringing into captivity every thought to the obedience of Christ."*

4) <u>Conscience</u>: Our conscience is the outer protection for our mind and soul. It is similar to a warning system to alert us to what is right and wrong. Our conscience alerts us to sin, but our conscience can be seared as stated in 1 Timothy 4:2. If we practice sinning, our discernment gradually decreases and our conscience has been seared and is no longer effective. God is an amazing Creator who gave us a conscience, but if we misuse this gift by continuing to practice sinning, we have removed a safeguard from our lives.

Fellowship with the LORD is essential for our wholeness. *"If we say that we have fellowship with Him, and walk in darkness, we lie and do not practice the truth. But if we walk in the light as He is in the light, we have fellowship with one another, and the blood of Jesus Christ His Son cleanses us from all sin"* (1 John 1:6-9). Abiding with the LORD will be our best life and will be an abundant life.

Jesus carried off our griefs, which are our sicknesses (Strong's Concordance), by His victory on the cross (Isaiah 53:4-5). The kingdom of darkness wants us sick in body, mind, and soul. God has given believers spiritual authority, through the power of the Holy Spirit, over the kingdom of darkness. The Holy Spirit breathes life into our being. *"But if the Spirit of Him who raised Jesus from the dead dwells in you, He who raised Christ from the dead will also give life to your mortal bodies through His Spirit who dwells in you"* (Romans 8:11).

Our thought life affects our wholeness in body, mind, and soul. Our thoughts are either from the Holy Spirit, ourselves, the world, or Satan. If our thoughts are from Satan or the world, they will be in opposition to the Word of God. If our thoughts are from the Holy Spirit, they will agree with the Word of God. We need to learn to discern the difference. If our thoughts are not agreeing with the Word of God, we must remove them and think on things that are based in truth.

The LORD wants us to prosper and be in health. When our heart and mind are at peace, our inner man is at peace. Your mind will be at peace when you are following the will of God. *"And be not conformed to this world but be transformed by the renewing of your mind, that you may prove what is good, and acceptable, and perfect will of God"* (Romans 12:2). When you guard your heart, your heart will be at peace. *"Keep your heart with all diligence; for out of it are the issues of life"* (Proverbs 4:23). According to 3 John 2, when our soul prospers, we will prosper and be in health.

What is the condition of your soul? If your soul is wounded, you need to be delivered/healed from your soul wound. The person with the wounded soul is more likely to listen to fleshly desires then the Holy Spirit. These wounds can be deep inside the soul, and we may not realize the wound remains. We can ask God to reveal to us any soul wounds that need to be dealt with. We can deal with our soul wounds by recognizing the truth from the situation; speak the truth about the experience; repent or forgive depending which applies; pray that through Jesus completed work on the cross, you are healed. With the power of the Holy Spirit, our soul is healed (Isaiah 53:5, Romans 8:11).

If sickness comes upon a person, God wants them healed. He is called <u>Jehovah-Rapha, God Who Heals</u>. III John 2 says, *"Beloved, I pray that you may prosper in all things and be in health, just as your soul prospers."* God's perfect plan for His people is that our souls prosper and that we be in health.

FEAR AND ITS DANGERS

God has an order for our wellbeing. We are to be doers of the Word of God by casting off our worry and trusting our daily life to the LORD. This is God's order for our lives. He has told us not to worry about tomorrow (Matthew 6:25-34).

If we live in anxiety, stress, fear, hostility, anger, self-bitterness, guilt, rage, or self-accusation, we have opened the door to error and darkness. *"A sound heart is the life of the flesh: but envy the rottenness of the bones"* (Proverbs 14:30). The pureness of our heart has a direct correlation to the pureness of our body. The LORD wants us to examine our hearts and keep them pure (Ephesians 4:31-32).

Fear can take over our lives if we allow it to. Perfect love casts out all fear. *"And I am convinced that nothing can ever separate us from God's love. Neither death nor life, neither angels nor demons, neither our fears for today nor our worries about tomorrow —not even the powers of hell can separate us from God's love. No power in the sky above or in the earth below—indeed, nothing in all creation will ever be able to separate us from the love of God that is revealed in Christ Jesus our LORD"* (Romans 8:38-39). God's love is so deep and so wide that fear must leave when we receive His love. When we have a personal relationship with the LORD and realize in our heart the depth of His love for us, then fear has no place in our heart.

God wants us to cast off our thoughts of fear. But we need to replace the fear with meditating on the word of God. By seeking God's truth in His word, we will build our faith. *"So then faith cometh by hearing and hearing by the word of God"* (Romans 10:17). Your faith will chase fear away (Joshua 1:8).

The lies of Satan bring destruction to our bodies. The world has told us that fear, stress, and anxiety can be managed by medication and psychotherapy. You can't manage fear. Fear is a spirit according to Second Timothy 1:7; the spirit of fear has to be removed. The word of God says we are not to worry. It is a sin to worry; therefore, we must repent and ask the LORD to restore us to health. Worry has ugly relatives and their names are fear, anxiety, stress, phobias, despair, horror, dismay, panic, fright, cowardice, timidity, and discouragement. God has an order in the way He created us. We were not created to fear and stress about life. We are created to trust Our Creator and rest in Him. Just like a plant needs sun and water to live, we need to trust in Our Creator to live and live life abundantly. *"Therefore humble yourselves under the mighty hand of God, that He may exalt you in due time, casting all your care upon Him, for He cares for you. Be sober, be vigilant; because your adversary the devil walks about like a roaring lion, seeking whom he may devour. Resist him, steadfast in the faith, knowing that the same sufferings are experienced by your brotherhood in the world. But may the God of all grace, who called us to His eternal glory by Christ Jesus, after you have suffered a while, perfect, establish, strengthen, and settle you. To Him be the glory and the dominion forever and ever. Amen"* (1 Peter 5:6-11). We are purified, established, and strengthened as we overcome and renounce the worries of this world.

PERSONAL TESTIMONY

"My people are destroyed for lack of knowledge: because you have rejected knowledge, I will also reject you, that you shall be no priest to Me: seeing you have forgotten the law of your God, I will also forget your children" (Hosea 4:6). Notice this scripture says "My people". Believers have been destroyed for lack of knowledge. I was oppressed with fear, and I did not recognize how it controlled my life. The sin of living in fear affected me and others in my life. Fear is contagious and so are many other sins. We can mimic other people's sinful behaviors and incorrect thought patterns. We can learn lies that create strongholds in our life that can oppress us. God's word says we are to pull down strongholds and every high thing that exalts itself against the knowledge of God (2 Corinthians 10:4-5). Fear was a stronghold in my life. Once I recognized the power I had given to fear, I made a decision to pull down this stronghold.

Fear can cause all kinds of medical symptoms in our bodies. It is amazing the lies fear tells our body. I had to confront fear in my life. First of all, I recognized fear as a liar. Secondly, I confronted and renounced fear. After my confession and repentance, I needed to replace fear with faith. If fear ever tries to knock on my door again, I need to slam the door on fear. I must continue standing in faith and not let fear get any access. I must keep all doors closed to fear.

THE FULLNESS OF THE BELIEVER

1) Salvation. Jesus Christ is the Son of the living God. The gospel is the good news that Jesus Christ came to earth as a man, died on the cross, paid the price for our sins, resurrected from the dead, ascended into heaven, and will return as the Judge of the earth. When we say we believe in Jesus Christ as our LORD and Savior, this means we trust Him, follow Him, and obey Him; we become His children and have everlasting life. *"For God so loved the world, that He gave His only begotten Son, that whosoever believes in Him should not perish, but have everlasting life"* (John 3:16).

"That if you shall confess with your mouth the LORD Jesus, and shall believe in your heart that God has raised Him from the dead, you shall be saved. For with the heart man believes to righteousness; and with the mouth confession is made to salvation" (Romans 10:9-10). When we believe in the redemptive work of Jesus Christ as the Son of the living God, we will respond by repenting of sin (change our mind); make a confession that Jesus Christ is LORD; obey Him; and remain faithful with godly sorrow which works repentance to salvation. Part of our obedience to God is being baptized (immersion). *"And now why tarriest (delay) you? Arise, and be baptized, and wash away your sins, calling on the name of the LORD"* (Acts 22:16). When we believe in Jesus Christ as our LORD and Savior, we trust Him, follow Him, and obey Him. Being baptized is obeying what God's word says. According to Mark 16:16, *"He that believes and is baptized shall be saved: but he that believes not shall be damned."* Also, I suggest reading Acts 2:38-47 to understand more fully the importance of our obedience and being baptized.

"Jesus answered and said to him, "Verily, verily, I say to you, Except a man be born again, he cannot see the kingdom of God" (John 3:3). Being born again is when God imparts eternal life to those who accept Jesus as their Savior and are dead in their sins. When you are born again, your spirit is resurrected from the dead. Your life radically changes when you are born again. We are no longer separated from God when we are born again. We are sealed by the Holy Spirit (Ephesians 1:13). When we are born again, the Holy Spirit will make us aware of sin, and we will be guided to the truth. A born again Christian believes that Jesus Christ is the Son of God and believes Jesus redemptive work on the cross is finished (Acts 8:36-38); and is drawn and led by the Holy Spirit (John 14:26), drawn to repentance, and is baptized (John 16:7-8,

Acts 2:38, Acts 22:16); and godly sorrow works repentance to salvation (2 Corinthians 7:9-10).

A born again believer:
    o <u>Confesses Christ</u> (Matthew 10:32, Romans 10:9-11).
    o <u>Is drawn and led by the Holy Spirit</u> (John 14:26).
    o <u>Drawn to repentance and baptized</u> (Acts 2:38-41, Acts 22:16, Matthew 28:19, Mark 16:16). Being baptized is part of our obedience. There may be circumstances where baptism is not possible like the thief on the cross (Luke 23:42-43). Being baptized is part of obeying God, and we need to be careful if we are choosing not to be baptized (immersion) because of disobedience. There was a time when I wasn't baptized by immersion, and I would tell myself things to justify not wanting to be baptized (immersion) for worldly reasons. When we obey God, we will need to step out of our comfort. There is power in baptism, and there is power in our obedience. Being baptized was part of the process for me being set free and born again! (Romans 6:3-4-baptism by immersion is a representation of dying to our old man when we go down in the water and are raised to new life when we come out of the water in baptism.)
    o <u>Has godly sorrow which works repentance to salvation</u> (2 Corinthians 7:9-10).
    o My born-again experience was a purification process as the Holy Spirit would reveal the truth to me, and I would need to respond in obedience.

An erring born again believer needs to: (as born again believers, we are not to practice sinning)
    o <u>Repent and pray</u> (Acts 8:21-23). Repent is to change one's mind.
    o <u>Confess sins</u> (1 John 1:9). Confession is to admit or declare yourself guilty.

Through the blood of Jesus, we are overcomers. As born again believers, we are not to practice sinning. When the Holy Spirit leads us to recognize sin, we are to repent (change one's mind), pray, and confess our sin (sorrowfully acknowledge our sin). We stand in faith and proclaim the victory we have over Satan by the power of the blood of Jesus and His victory on the cross. We declare and decree that through the blood of Jesus we are justified (just as if we never sinned) and are sanctified (made holy). Through the blood of Jesus, all my sins are forgiven, and I am redeemed out of the hand of Satan. Through the blood of Jesus, I have the boldness to come before God, and I am seated in heavenly places (Revelation 12:11, Hebrews 10:19).

2) Sanctification. As believers, we undergo a process of sanctification where we are made holy. The Greek definition of sanctification is making holy, set apart, holiness. Acts 26:18 explains sanctification, *"to open their (spiritual) eyes so that they may turn from darkness to light and from the power of Satan to God, that they may receive forgiveness and release from their sins and an inheritance among those who have been sanctified (set apart, made holy) by faith in Me."* Through sanctification, we see through our spiritual eyes the truth, and we will have a great hate for sin and will run to the light of Jesus Christ.

3) Baptism. The word baptism in the Greek language means "to immerse" and in Hebrew, it means "immersion". Therefore, when someone is baptized according to scripture, it is full immersion. As a born again believer, baptism (by immersion) is a sign of your obedience to the LORD. The following verses of Romans 6:4-7 are a great explanation of what baptism represents. *"Therefore we are buried with Him by baptism into death: that like as Christ was raised up from the dead by the glory of the Father, even so we also should walk in newness of life. For if we have been planted together in the likeness of His death, we shall be also in the likeness of His resurrection: knowing this, that our old man is crucified with Him, that the body of sin might be destroyed, that hereafter we should not serve sin. For he that is dead is freed from sin."* After we have accepted Jesus as our LORD and Savior, we are told in the Word of God to be baptized. Therefore, we are to be baptized by immersion once we believe in Jesus as our LORD and Savior.

4) Baptism of the Holy Spirit. *"And when Paul had laid his hand upon them, the Holy Ghost came on them; and they spake with tongues, and prophesied"* (Acts 19:6). When you speak in tongues, you edify yourself and prophesying edifies the church according to 1 Corinthians 14:4.

5) The LORD's Supper (Holy Communion). *"And He took bread, and gave thanks, and broke it, and gave to them, saying, 'This is My body which is given for you: this do in remembrance of Me.' Likewise also the cup after supper saying, 'This cup is the new testament in My blood, which is shed for you' "* (Luke 22:19-20). The LORD's Supper is the New Covenant (Testament) for those that believe and proclaim His death until He comes (1 Corinthians 11:26). On the cross, Jesus Christ paid the price for our sins, curses, and sicknesses. By Jesus's stripes, we are healed.

6) Greatest Commandment: We are to love God with all our heart, love ourselves, and love our neighbor. Recorded in Matthew 22:37-40, Jesus said unto him, *"Thou shalt love the LORD thy God with all they heart, and with all thy soul, and with all thy mind. This is the first and great commandment. And the second is like unto it, Thou shalt love thy neighbor as thyself. On these two commandments hang all the law and the prophets."*

7) Forgiveness. The LORD commands that we forgive ourselves and others, and remove all bad thoughts towards others (Matthew 6:14-15).

8) Believer's **walk by faith**, not fear. *"For we walk by faith, not by sight"* (2 Corinthians 5:7).

9) We can't conform to the patterns of this world, but we need to renew our minds with the Word of God. We will need to watch what activities we do, who we spend time with, and what we let into our minds and hearts (Romans 12:2).

10) Obedience to the LORD is not a suggestion, it is a command. **The Holy Spirit leads us to repentance**. *"For as many as are led by the Spirit of God, they are the sons of God"* (Romans 8:14). (Jeremiah 26:13)

11) *"**Submit yourselves therefore to God**. Resist the devil, and he will flee from you. Draw near to God, and He will draw near to you. Cleanse your hands, you sinners; and purify your hearts, you double minded. Be afflicted, and mourn, and weep; let your laughter be turned to mourning, and your joy to heaviness. Humble yourselves in the sight of the LORD, and He shall lift you up"* (James 4:7-10).

12) *"I am the vine, you are the branches, he who abides in Me, and I in him, he bears much fruit, for apart from Me you can do nothing"* (John 15:5). In your lifelong walk with the LORD, you will want to **spend daily time in the Word of God and prayer**. Seek God's knowledge (Word of God), not the knowledge of the world. The truth will set you free (John 8:31-32, Hebrews 4:12). You will want to **be part of a full gospel church and Bible study group.**

13) In Isaiah 58, the LORD teaches us how to **Fast and Pray**. In these scriptures, He says we should **serve and help those in need.** In doing this, we will loose the bands of wickedness, and the oppressed will be set free.

14) Praise God in all circumstances. When your focus is on your Almighty God, His goodness and His power, the darkness loses its grip (John 4:23-24).

15) *"For whatsoever a man sows, that shall he also reap"* (Galatians 6:7-8). When we sow worldly things into our flesh, we will reap corruption. For example; what choices are we making, what do we let our eyes see and our ears hear, what do we put into our bodies, what words do we speak, what thoughts do we meditate on, what do we spend our time doing, etc. When we sow good things including the Word of God into our being, we will reap good fruit.

GOD WANTS YOU HEALED, DELIVERED, AND MADE WHOLE. HE WANTS YOU DISCHARGED FROM THE HOSPITAL (DISCHARGED FROM THE LIES YOU ONCE BELIEVED). HE WANTS YOU SET FREE TO HAVE THE ABUNDANT LIFE AND WALK INTO THE PLANS HE HAS FOR YOUR LIFE!

PERSONAL TESTIMONY

For about six years, I worked in a counseling center with a psychologist, psychiatrist, and social workers. I transcribed the psychologist's notes. The psychologist cared very much for the wellness of his patients. The thing that always troubled me was how people never seemed to be set free from their problems. Most of the patients went to continued counseling for many years. When the word of God and God's plans for the person are not appropriated into their life, how can people receive their wholeness and overcome? The world's way is to manage problems, but God's way is to set people free. The counselor who helps the patient appropriate God's plan and God's word into their life can find victory and freedom versus managing an issue for a lifetime.

CHAPTER 19

Laying on of Hands

The laying on of hands is a means given to us by God to bring His kingdom to earth. We as believers are authorized to lay hands on the sick, in the name of Jesus, and the sick will recover. When Jesus commissioned His disciples to go into the world and preach the gospel, Jesus also told them to lay hands on the sick. Jesus was the example for His disciples to follow. In Matthew 8:3, Jesus touched a man with leprosy, and he was healed. In Luke 13:12-13, Jesus laid hands on a woman and said to her *"woman you are loosed from your infirmity"* and she was made straight. Those that have accepted the call to be Jesus's disciples today, on the earth, are to: *"lay hands on the sick, and they shall recover"* according to Mark 16:14-18.

The laying on of hands in faith is also used to impart a blessing. In Matthew 19:13-15, Jesus had children come to Him, and He laid hands on them to bless them. A husband and wife can lay hands on their children and bless them. A Pastor can lay hands on children to impart a blessing, as their parents bring them forward, to dedicate them to the LORD. These are just some examples (Genesis 48:14).

The LORD had Moses lay his hands on Joshua in Numbers 27:18-23. The LORD told Moses to take Joshua before the priest and the congregation, and Joshua would be commissioned. Joshua was going to lead the children of Israel into the Promised Land. God told Moses to lay hands on Joshua and that some of Moses' honor would go to Joshua. This imparted a blessing on Joshua as the leader of the Israelites. Joshua was blessed by God to lead them into the Promised Land.

The laying on of hands, in faith, is also for the baptism of the Holy Spirit and imparting blessings of the Holy Spirit. In Acts 8:17, they laid hands on them to receive the Holy Spirit. Additionally in Acts 19:6, Paul laid his hands on them, and the Holy Spirit came on them, and they spoke in tongues and prophesied. My personal testimony of a similar experience was when two believers laid hands on me, for the baptism of the Holy Spirit, I spoke in tongues that day. This blessing was very powerful in my life, as it empowered me to understand God's truth with more clarity. It gave me a boldness and discernment that I didn't have before.

The laying on of hands in faith will create signs and wonders. In Mark 8, the disciples brought a blind man to Jesus. Jesus put spit on the blind man's eyes and laid His hands on him. The blind man stated his vision wasn't clear so Jesus touched his eyes a second time. The man's eyesight was now restored completely. Jesus has commissioned those who believe to lay hands on the sick, and they will recover (Acts 5:12-16).

There was a handyman working at my home, and he had told me he had metal in his shoulder, back, and arm because of an injury. He was in pain and had limited movement. The work he was doing at my home was completed, and I asked him if I could pray for him. I was surprised when he said yes because I knew nothing about what he believed. I laid hands on his back and shoulder and prayed "you are made new and healed in the name of Jesus". He texted me a few weeks later to wish me a Merry Christmas and told me that he felt good, and he had no pain. I was extremely blessed to have the opportunity to pray for Kevin and witness the power of God that day.

The laying on of hands needs to be done with care. The laying on of hands should not be done as a ritual or for palm reading (Deuteronomy 18:10). In addition, recorded in First Timothy 5:22, *"Lay hands suddenly on no man, neither be partakers of other men's sins: keep thyself pure."* The laying on of hands is spiritually powerful and should be done thoughtfully.

PERSONAL TESTIMONY

Many years ago, I started laying hands on my own body for healing. The Holy Spirit led me to lay hands on my body for continued health and healing. I knew that in the Bible it said, *"they will lay hands on the sick, and they will recover"* (Mark 16:18). I had never heard anyone teach on this before but felt led by the Holy Spirit. Years later, I had heard two different teachers speak about laying hands on yourself for healing. If I am willing to go to the physician's office and wait to see the doctor, why also wouldn't I be willing to spend the time waiting on my Almighty God for my continued health and healing with the laying on of hands?

CHAPTER 20

Relationships Built on Solid Ground

Love is the basis for our relationships to be built on solid ground. We are to love the LORD our God above all else. Secondly, we are to love our neighbor as ourselves. Therefore, solid relationships start with loving God first, loving ourselves, and loving our fellow man.

Many of our relationships will require self-sacrificing love. John 15:13 says, *"Greater love has no one than this: to lay down one's life for one's friends."* 1 Corinthians 13:4-6 says, *"Love suffers long and is kind; love does not envy; loves does not parade itself, is not puffed up; does not behave rudely, does not seek its own, is not provoked, thinks no evil; does not rejoice in iniquity, but rejoices in the truth; bears all things, believes all things, hopes all things, endures all things."* Having this kind of love is required of us. This kind of love will mature us and purify us. An example of this love is in the Book of Ruth. The story begins with the Israelite family of Naomi and Elimelech. They have two sons, and they leave Bethlehem to go to Moab because of a famine. Naomi's husband Elimelech dies. Naomi's sons marry Moabite women; Ruth and Orpah. Then her two sons died. Now Naomi,

Ruth, and Orpah have no husbands. Naomi has decided to go back to Bethlehem and tells her daughters-in-law to go back to their mother's homes in Moab. Therefore, Orpah leaves to go back to her mother's home in Moab, but Ruth clung to Naomi. Ruth says to Naomi, "*. . . for where you go, I will go; and where you lodge, I will lodge: your people shall be my people, and your God my God. . .*" Therefore, Naomi and Ruth went to Bethlehem together. These women went from heartbreak to wholeness. Ruth's steps of faith and self-sacrificing love led to her having a new life that also blessed Naomi. Ruth met and married Boaz, a Hebrew man. They had a son, and this son was the grandfather of King David. God moved this family into their promised inheritance of the Messiah being born through their family line. This story is not only a story of self-sacrificing love but a story of how God redeems the lives of the brokenhearted.

God wants us to be wise in choosing our friendships and relationships. Being unequally yoked with an unbeliever in marriage or a close friendship can cause us to stumble. Sin can get a foothold on us through ungodly relationships. We need to agree with God and His best for our life. *"Be you not unequally yoked together with unbelievers: for what fellowship has righteousness with unrighteousness? And what communion has light with darkness?" (*2 Corinthians 6:14).

God ordained marriage to be between a man and a woman. Marriage is of great value to God; therefore, it should be of great value to us. Additionally, Hebrews 13:4 states that sexually immoral and adulterers will be judged by God. Anything done outside of God's order, we open ourselves up to trouble. We are to war against fornication by fighting for our purity in relationships. When we agree with God's order, we are protecting ourselves. The Holy Spirit gives us the self-control we need to be obedient to God (Genesis 2:24, 1 Thessalonians 4:3).

God has a distinct order in the family. God made the husband head of the household. The husband is head of the wife as Christ is the head of the church. God has placed the husband over the wife to protect her. If our spouse is rebelling against God's marital order, release them to God in prayer and ask God to change their heart to be obedient to God (Proverbs 21:1). When we stay obedient to God and let God work on the other person, this is when we will see the power of God operate in our marriage (Ephesians 5:22-33).

If someone is in our life that leads us into temptation or causes us to sin, we need to carefully and seriously evaluate the relationship. Be wary of relationships of manipulation and control. God gives us free will, and we should not be manipulated into someone else's evil. Additionally, we need to be wary of jealousy and envy. In Proverbs 14:30, this verse speaks about how envy makes the bones rot. According to James 3:16, this verse explains how jealousy and selfish ambition will cause disorder and every vile practice. We need to flee from envy and jealousy. We need to go to God for wisdom and direction in these difficult relationships. If we are in a relationship where we are more worried about pleasing that person then pleasing God, this person can cause us to stumble. We need to be careful we don't place any person above God, and they become our idol. We are not to fear man but fear God (Matthew 10:26-28).

According to Matthew 10:36, *". . . and a man's enemies will be those of his own household."* We need to be cautious of any relationship whether friend or family that is unhealthy and could cause us to stumble into sin. God's word says in 1 Corinthians 15:33, *"Do not be deceived: Evil company corrupts good habits."* We may need to limit time with someone that is causing us to stumble. Pray to God for wisdom in these relationships.

In our relationships, we are to speak the truth in love. The truth makes people free. Speaking the truth in love is required of us. When people are going through trials and temptations, God may use us to speak truth to them. Pray that God gives you the words to speak in love.

In Ecclesiastes 3, it speaks of seasons in life and how there is a purpose and time for all things. Verse 6 states, *"A time to get, and a time to lose; a time to keep, and a time to cast away."* There are some friendships that are only for a season. Situations in life change and certain friendships seem to have an ending point, and it is best to let those friendships end.

God has placed authorities in our lives, and we are to submit to those authorities. God placed the father as the head of the household. We have various other leaders and authorities in our lives. Without authorities, there would be chaos. Furthermore, every knee must bow to Jesus and answer to Jesus our Judge. Therefore, vengeance is the LORD's and any leader doing evil will answer to the Almighty. If you are in a situation where your leader is putting you in a position where you are asked to engage in or be part of evil, pray to the LORD to show you the way out of the situation according to 1 Corinthians 10:13. He is faithful and will show you the way of escape (Hebrews 13:17, 1 Peter 2:13-21). About twenty years ago, there was a situation at work where a male co-worker put his hands on me inappropriately and made inappropriate remarks. I was frozen in fear when it happened. I never told anyone for a long time. Back in my younger years, I didn't know my true identity and my worth. As I processed what had happened, I knew my employer would be angry and probably fire him. I knew if I told my husband he would be upset. Back then, I didn't deal with confrontation very well so I kept it to myself. God placed my husband head of our household to protect me, and my employer was the authority at my job and was placed there to protect me. They were placed there as my covering. What I should have done was tell my employer and my husband. With truth, there will be confrontation because you are confronting the enemy. God teaches us how to confront the lies with the truth, in love.

After reading the above paragraphs on relationships and by reviewing the below scriptures, evaluate the relationships in your life. Determine those relationships that are healthy and those that are not. Pray to the LORD and ask for wisdom on setting boundaries for the unhealthy relationships and asking God if any of your unhealthy relationships need to end. The LORD is the Judge and judgment is His, but we are told to discern and know right from wrong, and good from evil. "... **You shall not be afraid of the face of man; for the judgment is God's and the cause that is too hard for you, bring it to me, and I will hear it**" (Deuteronomy 1:7).

SCRIPTURES FOR RELATIONSHIPS BUILT ON SOLID GROUND:

"Walk with the wise and become wise, for a companion of fools suffers harm" (Proverbs 13:20).

"Greater love has no one than this: to lay down one's life for one's friends" (John 15:13).

"And let us consider how we may spur one another on toward love and good deeds, not giving up meeting together, as some are in the habit of doing, but encouraging one another—and all the more as you see the Day approaching" (Hebrews 10:24-25).

"Be completely humble and gentle; be patient, bearing with one another in love. Make every effort to keep the unity of the Spirit through the bond of peace" (Ephesians 4:2-3).

"Do not be yoked together with unbelievers. For what do righteousness and wickedness have in common? Or what fellowship can light have with darkness?" (2 Corinthians 6:14)

"One who has unreliable friends soon comes to ruin, but there is a friend who sticks closer than a brother" (Proverbs 18:24).

"Flee from sexual immorality. All other sins a person commits are outside the body, but whoever sins sexually, sins against their own body" (1 Corinthians 6:18).

"Pride goes before destruction, and a haughty spirit before a fall" (Proverbs 16:18).

"An ungodly man digs up evil: and in his lips there is as a burning fire. A forward (perverse) man sows strife: and a whisperer separates chief friends. A violent man

entices his neighbor, and leads him into the way that is not good" (Proverbs 16:27-29).

"Keep your heart with all diligence; for out of it are the issues of life" (Proverbs 4:23).

"Love is to be sincere and active (the real thing—without guile and hyprocrisy). Hate what is evil (detest all ungodliness, do not tolerate wickedness); hold on tightly to what is good. Be devoted to one another with (authentic) brotherly affection (as members of one family), give preference to one another in honor" (Romans 12:9-10).

"Love endures with patience and serenity, love is kind and thoughtful, and is not jealous or envious; love does not brag and is not proud or arrogant. It is not rude; it is not self-seeking, it is not provoked (nor overly sensitive and easily angered); it does not take into account a wrong endured. It does not rejoice at injustice, but rejoices with the truth (when right and truth prevail), Love bears all things (regardless of what comes), believes all things (looking for the best in each one), hopes all things (remaining steadfast during difficult times), endures all things (without weakening)" (1 Corinthians 13:4-7).

"Fulfill you my joy, that you be likeminded, having the same love, being of one accord, of one mind. Let nothing be done through strife or vain glory; but in lowliness of mind let each esteem other better than themselves. Look not every man on his own things, but every man also on the things of others" (Philippians 2:2-4).

"For this is the will of God, even your sanctification, that you should abstain from fornication" (1 Thessalonians 4:3).

"That no man go beyond and defraud his brother in any matter: because that the LORD is the avenger of all such, as we also have forewarned you and testified. For God has not called us to uncleanness, but to holiness" (1 Thessalonians 4:6-7).

"Wherefore comfort yourselves together, and edify one another, even as also you do" (1 Thessalonians 5:11).

"Prove all things; hold fast that which is good. Abstain from all appearance of evil" (1 Thessalonians 5:21-22).

"Therefore let us not sleep, as do others; but let us watch and be sober. For they that sleep in the night; and they that be drunken are drunken in the night. But let us, who are of the day, be sober; putting on the breastplate of faith and love; and for a helmet, the hope of salvation" (1 Thessalonians 5:6-8).

As you evaluate your relationships, you are also evaluating yourself in those relationships. The scriptures above will help you not only pinpoint problem relationships but problems you may be causing or contributing to. Seek God's guidance for direction on how to do a course adjustment. *"Confess your faults one to another, and pray one for another, that you may be healed . . ."* (James 5:16). We are responsible for our part in a relationship. We cannot make that choice for someone else, but we can pray for them.

CHAPTER 21

Truth Changes Fact

The fact was the wages of sin was death. Jesus came to earth and through His death on the cross He overcame sin, curses, sickness, death, and Satan, and we now have eternal life through our faith in Jesus as our LORD and Savior. Truth changed the fact.

The fact may be that some people have brokenness in their body, mind, or soul, but the truth is our Heavenly Father heals the brokenhearted and binds up their wounds. Truth changes the fact. (Psalm 147:3).

The fact may be some people are in need. Our Heavenly Father supplies every need according to His riches. Go to God in prayer. Go supply someone else's need. His truth changes the fact (Philippians 4:19).

The fact may be some people are oppressed by Satan. The Word of God says to submit to God, resist Satan, and Satan will flee. With our obedience to God, we are set free. Truth and obedience to God move oppression out of our lives. Truth changes the fact (James 4:7).

The fact was in Luke 13:11-13 there was a woman who for 18 years had an evil spirit causing her to be bent over. Jesus saw her and said to her, *"Woman you are loosed from your infirmity."* Jesus laid His hands on her and she stood straight. Truth changed 18 years of facts.

The fact was in Luke 8:43-48 that a woman had a bleeding problem for 12 years. She touched the garment of Jesus. Jesus said to her, *"Daughter be of good comfort: your faith has made you whole; go in peace."* The fact was for 12 years she suffered, but with the power of Jesus and faith, truth prevailed and her facts changed in a moment.

The fact was that Jairus's daughter died (Luke 8:41-56), Lazarus died ((John 11), and Jesus died (John 19-20). The truth is they all rose from the dead. Truth changes the fact, and Jesus's death and resurrection changed everything. Truth brings the dead back to life.

The facts may be that you lost years of your life from disobeying God. The truth is God wants to set you free and turn your life around. Submit to God and your life will be redeemed. God's truth changes your facts. God's truth is He wants you to confess and repent, and He remembers your sin no more. That is the truth!

The fact is there are a lot of people not saved, not getting their needs met, not healed, not delivered, and not set free. The truth is God has a plan for you to help people know Jesus, to help people get their needs met, to help people be healed, to help people get delivered, and to help people be set free! When you walk into the plans God has for you to help others, truth shows up when you show up, and the captives are set free!

The fact is Satan tries to steal, kill, and destroy our families. But the truth is God can redeem the lost years. According to Joel 2:25, *"And I will restore to you the years that the locust has eaten."* What scripture verse are you standing on for your family? Your faith will change your current facts into your future victory!

The fact is I did not find out the full truth from sitting in a church pew. I had to actively seek God for His truth. The Word of God says that when I ask, I will be given; when I seek, I will find; and when I knock, it shall be opened to me. I wanted the truth from God and He gave me the truth!

Truth restores, truth brings hope, truth heals, truth shows the way out, truth delivers, truth brings the dead back to life, truth . . . . What has the truth done in your life?!!

Truth in my life has purified my faith, removed fear, made me free, brought me peace, healed me, delivered me, and led me to make changes in my life for God.

TRUTH CHANGES PEOPLE AND SITUATIONS. IF YOU SEE NO CHANGE, SEEK TRUTH. GOD CHANGES PEOPLE AND SITUATIONS. IF YOU WANT CHANGE IN YOUR LIFE, KEEP SEEKING THE LORD FOR THE TRUTH, AND HE WILL MOVE YOU INTO A BETTER LIFE. IT IS VERY FREEING WHEN YOU ALLOW GOD TO LEAD YOU INTO THE UNKNOWN. WHEN WE HOLD ONTO

WHAT WE LEARNED IN THE PAST AND NEVER ALLOW GOD TO REVEAL NEW THINGS TO US, WE STOP GROWING SPIRITUALLY. WE ARE SPIRIT BEINGS WHO LONG TO GROW IN CHRIST AND HIS TRUTH.

BIBLIOGRAPHY

Biblegateway.com. 2018. Kings James Version, New King James Version, Amplified Bible.

Biblehub.com. Strong's Concordance by Helps Ministries, Inc. 2011.

Biblehub.com. Thayer's Greek Lexicon by Biblesoft, Inc. 2011.

Biblehub.com. NAS Exhaustive Concordance of the Bible with Hebrew-Aramaic of the Bible with Hebrew and Greek Dictionaries. Lockman Foundation. 1988.

Brooks, Steven. *How to Operate in the Gifts of the Spirit*. Shippensburg, PA: Destiny Image Publishers, Inc., 2014.

Dictionary.com. 2019.

Ewing, Minister Kevin L.A. "Understanding the Mystery of Fasting". YouTube.

"Forgiveness: Letting Go of Grudges and Bitterness". Healthy Lifestyle Adult Health. Mayo Foundation for Medical Education & Research. 2019.

"Forgiveness: Your Health Depends on It". John Hopkins Medicine. 2019.

GodRules.net. KJV Strong's Concordance.

Guetzo, Allen C. (April 12, 2012). "The Pride Before the Titanic's Fall." The New York Post.

King James Version Easy Reading Bible. Goodyear, AZ: The Publisher, 2002.

Mayfield, Margy. Margy "Mayfield Abduction Testimony". SEEK4TRUTH.TK. YouTube.

Merriam-Webster Dictionary. www.merriam-webster.com. Since 1828.

Price, Frederick K. C. *Answered Prayer Guaranteed*. Lake Mary, Florida: Charisma House. 2006.

Prince, Derek. *They Shall Expel Demons*. Grand Rapids, MI: Chosen Books. 1998.

Scrivner, Thurman. The Living Savior Ministries. CD Healing Teachings. Justin, TX.

Smith, Michael W. HardcoreChristianity.com. YouTube Deliverance Training Videos. Sun City, AZ.

"The Deadly Consequences of Unforgiveness". Lorie Johnson. CBN News. June 22, 2015.

Winston, Dr. Bill. *Transform Your Thinking, Transform Your Life*. Tulsa, OK: Harrison House, Inc. 2008.

Wommack, Andrew. *The New You and the Holy Spirit*. Colorado Springs, CO: Andrew Wommack Industries, Inc., 2012.

Wright, Dr. Henry W. *A More Excellent Way*. New Kensington, PA: Whitaker House, 2009.

ABOUT AUTHOR

DENISE WHITE has been married for 31 years and has two children. Denise is a follower of Jesus Christ. Her faith has brought her peace and victory. Denise has a B.S. Degree and is a member of Delta Mu Delta. She has enjoyed her career in educating children. Denise's ministries have included ministering in the marketplace, children's groups, homeless women, and foster care ministry.

ABOUT KHARIS PUBLISHING

Kharis Publishing, an imprint of Kharis Media LLC, is a leading inspirational and faith publisher with a core mission to publish impactful books, and support at-risk children with literacy tools.

Kharis Publishing has partnered with AuthorClearance.Com, a major direct-to-consumer (D2C) distribution platform, to help authors build a following, grow their brand, and sell more books. As an author, Kharis will publish your book for free, give you 50% discount off all author copies, provide a free online store with ecommerce and social networking tools to help you build a community around your title and sell even more books. Absolutely free. Learn more at www.authorclearance.com.